# THE
# DISPOSSESSED
# GARDEN

# THE DISPOSSESSED GARDEN

*Pastoral and History in
Southern Literature*

LEWIS P. SIMPSON

*MERCER UNIVERSITY LAMAR
MEMORIAL LECTURES, NO. 16*

UNIVERSITY OF GEORGIA PRESS

ATHENS

❧

©

1975

THE UNIVERSITY OF GEORGIA PRESS

Athens 30602

Library of Congress Catalog Card Number: 74–80942

International Standard Book Number: 0–8203–0355–0

*Printed in the United States of America*

"The Southern Recovery of Memory and History" appeared in the *Sewanee Review*, LXXXII (Winter 1974). A few changes have been made in the essay as it appears in this volume.

For
Thomas A. Kirby

*And yf that olde bokes were aweye,*
*Yloren were of remembraunce the keye.*

# Contents

# *Foreword*

THE ENGLISH SETTLERS BROUGHT ACROSS THE ATLANTIC
an idea, a myth. Whether articulated in verse, fiction, and
sermons or borne at unconscious levels, the myth
proposed that America was the new Garden of Eden,
where mankind had a second chance to escape history.
Civilized Europe had failed, but in the New World, in the
new Garden, man as a new Adam would begin again.
This was the errand into the wilderness: the gnostic idea
of the New World as redemptive garden. The myth was
pastoral, in that it emphasized the garden or the wilderness, and it was a myth of innocence, in that the settlers
regarded themselves as God's chosen people.

The myth remains with us and within us, and still
influences virtually every area of American life. Nostalgi-
cally and sentimentally we idealize our various "Golden
Ages," the bygone days of presumed simplicity and
purity. We live in the semipastoral suburbs, or we flee
to rural communes, or even while trapped in the Ap-
palachias and black ghettoes of large cities we sing songs
of "Down Home," songs about "Yesterday." Reaction-
aries or reformers, blacks or whites, rich or poor, we are
bound together in our double-faced devotion to pastoralism and modernity.

Recently students of American experience have begun
to suggest this to us and to examine the origins and the
maintenance of the myth. Lewis P. Simpson, in this distinguished contribution to the Mercer University Lamar
Memorial Lectures, offers an interpretation of the South-

ern literary imagination's involvement in the myth. That
involvement was complicated by the presence of chattel
slavery in the South, and Professor Simpson illuminates
both the attempt of Southern writers to incorporate
chattel slavery into the pastoral myth and the consequences of the inevitable failure of that contradictory
attempt.

Professor Simpson's study, because of its originality
and importance, bears comparison with the very best
work that has been done in the field of myth and the
American experience. The Lamar Lectures Committee
and its friends are especially pleased that the Lamar Lectures at Mercer provided the forum for, and were graced
by, Professor Simpson's able and profound scholarship.
Eugenia Dorothy Blount Lamar, whose generous be-
quest made the lectures possible, desired that they provide "lectures of the very highest type of scholarship"
to aid in the study and preservation of Southern culture.
Professor Simpson's performance, we believe, is a fulfillment of that purpose.

> Michael Cass
> For the Lamar Lectures Committee

Mercer University
Macon, Georgia

# *Preface*

THIS SMALL VOLUME REPRESENTS AN ATTEMPT—LIMITED in perspective and highly selective in materials—to inquire into some aspects of the relationship between the pastoral sensibility and the historical sensibility as these may be discovered in the literature of the American South. Originally delivered at Mercer University on November 5–6, 1973 as the sixteenth series of the Eugenia Dorothy Blount Lamar Memorial Lectures, the three parts of the study are offered substantially as they were read as lectures.

I am indebted to the Lamar Lecture Committee for the honor of the invitation to join a distinguished company of lecturers. I wish to thank in particular President Rufus C. Harris, Dean Garland F. Taylor, and Professors Spencer B. King, Jr., Kenneth Hammond, John E. Byron, and Michael Cass for their truly gratifying hospitality during my visit to the Mercer campus.

Lewis P. Simpson

Louisiana State University, Baton Rouge
March 22, 1974

tionaries to modernity. The settlements they made in a "new world" were in one way or another responses to the dispossession of the integral and authoritative community of an "old world" by modern history. If they sowed the New World gardens with the seeds of modernity, the initial makers of these gardens did so unwittingly. They intended to make their new homes in Massachusetts and Virginia—save of course for their possible destruction by the hand of Providence—places of permanence, not jumping-off places for somewhere else. This at any rate is what the Massachusetts and Virginia plantings are conceived to be in the writings of those who attempted to imagine what these novel places meant. And it is with the imaginative constructs of Massachusetts and Virginia—with the possibilities of life in these places as idealized reactions to modernity—that I am broadly concerned in the first part of a brief and rather generalized inquiry into the subject of pastoral and history in Southern literature. I suggest that in a contrast between these idealized reactions we may define two fundamental versions of American pastoral: a New England "garden of the covenant" and a Southern "garden of the chattel." In the second part of my inquiry I comment on the endeavor of the literary mind of the antebellum South to accommodate a reactionary pastoral image of a slaveholders' world to the novel historical actuality of this world; and I point to the literary consequences of this effort, especially as these relate to an experience of alienation and dispossession in the Southern literary imagination. In the third part of my study of pastoral and history in Southern literature I attempt to comment on the connection between the antebellum Southern experience of an alienation from modernity and the mind of the twentieth-century Southern Renaissance, seeing this primarily in the replacement of the pastoral image in the Southern literary mind by a symbolism of memory and history.

Perhaps the best knowledge of the Puritan intention in coming to New England appears in John Winthrop's "A Modell of Christian Charity," a sermon Winthrop preached aboard the *Arbella* in 1630 as the first settlers of the Bay Colony were crossing the Atlantic. Winthrop told his fellow emigrants that "the cause between God and vs" is "a Covenant with Him" for the work of a planting in New England; and Winthrop prophesies both the reward for faithfulness to the covenant and the results of breaking it:

> Wee shall finde that the God of Israell is among vs, when tenn of vs shall be able to resist a thousand of our enemies, when hee shall make vs a prayse and glory, that men shall say of succeeding plantacions: the lord make it like that of New England. for wee must Consider that wee shall be as a City vpon a Hill, the eies of all people are uppon vs; soe that if wee shall deal falsely with our god in this worke wee haue vndertaken and soe cause him to withdrawe His present help from vs, we shall be made a story and a by-word through the world.[1]

But if it was to become famous, the image of New England as city on hill—the New Jerusalem of the Second Coming—was no more germane to the early New England imagination than the image of New England as a unique version of pastoral—a garden (or a vineyard) enclosed against a wilderness (or desert), which with some degree of poetic license we may call the garden of the covenant.[2] This metaphorical garden bears a kind of approximate connection with classical pastoral through an association in the Puritan mind between a mission to recover the purity of the initial age of Christianity and the migrant generation of New Englanders. Cotton Mather makes the association in his epic depiction of New England in the seventeenth century, *Magnalia Christi Americana* (1702). This begins with a self-conscious echo of the *Aeneid:* "I write the wonders of the Christian religion, flying from the depravations of Europe to the American strand; and, assisted by the holy author of that religion, I . . . report the wonderful displays of His infinite power, wisdom, goodness, and faithfulness, wherewith His divine providence hath irradiated an Indian wilderness." Mather proceeds confidently to compare the irradiation of the wasteland of the New World and the restoration of a golden age, not that of the classical writings, but that set forth in the lives and writings of the first Christians. His authority is no less a scholar than Peter Ramus.

> Thus I do not say [Mather declares] that the churches of New England are the most regular that can be, yet I do say, and am sure, that they are very like unto those that were in the first ages of Christianity. And if I assert that in the reformation of the church, the state of it in those ages is not a little to be considered, the great Peter Ramus, among others, has emboldened me. For when the Cardinal of Lorrain, the Maecaenas of the great man, was offended at him for turning Protestant, he replied, "Among those riches with which you enriched me, this I was mindful of always . . . . that of the fifteen centuries since Christ, the first is truly golden. The rest, the farther they are removed from the first, are the more worthless and degenerate. Therefore when choice was to be made I chose the golden age." In short, the first age was the golden one; to return unto that will make a man a Protestant, and I may add, a Puritan.[3]

But the chief reference for the Puritans—their major image of the mission of New England as the restoration of pure Christianity—was the story of the Israelites of the Exodus. God led the biblical people out of a land of bondage into a wilderness, which he transformed into a land of plenty. So he led the Puritan band out of the land of Archbishop Laud into "the dark regions of America," which were made into a land of plenty.

> And now the wilderness and the solitary place is glad for them; the desert rejoices and blossoms as a rose; it blossoms abundantly with peace and righteousness; it rejoices with joy and singing. . . . The waters of the divine influence break out in the wilderness and the streams in the desert; the parched ground becomes a pool and the thirsty land, springs of water; in the habitations of dragons where they lay there grows up the grass, and an high way now is there which is call'd the way of holiness over which the unclean do not pass and the wayfaring men do not err therein.

I am quoting from Thomas Prince's *A Sermon Delivered at Cambridge before the Great and General Assembly of the Province of Massachusetts* in 1730. This is an Election Day sermon, one in a succession of sermons delivered annually in Massachusetts from 1634 to 1884 on the occasion of the convening of the General Court. In these sermons— the best of which provide an indispensable record of "the New England way"—the purpose for many years was to call upon New Englanders to consider whether or not they were being faithful to the mission of the covenanted garden, to admonish them for backsliding, and to warn them of the consequences, as Prince said, of "great and dangerous declensions." [4] These had early been evident. In fact, by the time the New England garden had begun to be dotted with the graves of its first inhabitants, the priests of the garden saw serious defections from the holy purpose of New England. In 1670

Samuel Danforth declared in an Election Day sermon
that New Englanders were beginning to "abate and cool
in their affection to the pure worship of God which they
went into the wilderness to enjoy." And he asks New
Englanders to "call to remembrance the former days and
consider whether it was not then better with us than it
is now." But Danforth, it must be remarked, does not
invoke a nostalgic yearning for the good old days. His
purpose is to inquire "whether we have not in great
measure forgotten our errand into the wilderness." He
reminds his congregation in the General Court that "the
cause of leaving your country . . . and transporting
yourself over the vast ocean into this waste and howling
wilderness was . . . your enjoyment of the pure worship
of God according to his institution without human mix-
ture and impositions." Danforth's purpose is stern: to
exhort New Englanders to heed the warnings Jeremiah
gave the Israelites when they began to worship idols—to
consider "Israel apostasized and fallen." [5] Indeed Danforth's *A Brief Recognition of New England's Errand into the
Wilderness* may be said to announce what for many years
was a major theme of the Election Day sermons: the
falling off of a present generation from the dedicated
mission of the past generation or generations, and the
consequent threatened loss of the presence of God in the
vineyard or garden He had walled about his followers in
the wilderness. Forty years later the son of the preacher
who delivered *Errand into the Wilderness* gave one of the
most vivid of the "errand sermons" in *An Exhortation to
All to Use the Utmost Endeavours to Obtain a Visit of the God
of Hosts, for the Preservation of Religion, and the Church, upon
Earth.* Taking his text from Psalms 80:14 ("Return, we
beseech thee, O God of Hosts: look down from heaven,
and behold, and visit this vine"), the second Danforth
observed that "God the Father hath engaged himself to

be the Husbandman when Christ condescends to be the vine" and that "the invisible Church of the elect are likened to a vine or vineyard—they are the branches ingrafted into Christ."

> It is [Danforth II says] an intellectual, mystical vineyard— the mystical paradise of God, partly in heaven and partly on earth. As God planted an earthly paradise in the garden of Eden which did excel all the rest of the earth, so since the ruin of mankind by Adam's apostasy God will have a remnant among fallen mankind in every age and generation to be his vineyard, garden, orchard (or Eden, Eccles. 2:5), depending on and united unto Christ the second Adam.[6]

Without making an explicit identification of New England with the saving remnant, or the elect, who became the garden of God upon Adam's apostasy, Danforth skillfully plays upon the metaphor of the New England garden. As A. M. Plumstead observes in his admirable edition of New England Election Day sermons, Danforth makes a powerful comment on the presence of God, offering an interpretation of this not, as so often was done, in terms of a contractual arrangement but in the poetry of vision.[7] It is a vision both ecstatic and dread. He sees the "Divine visitation" of the vineyard, and yet he sees the converse, the "absence and withdrawing of God from his vineyard," with the result that "all things are out of order therein."

> When the master and owner of a garden is long absent, fences and hedges soon decay and the garden and the orchard yields little fruit for want of digging, pruning, weeding, and other good husbandry which the master's eye and presence would from time to time carefully bestow upon it. The sins of God's visible people provoke him to hide himself from them, yea to forsake us; and

when we lose the gracious presence of God, we soon lose
both our piety and prosperity. . . . After Israel forsook
the Lord . . . the land of Canaan which God gave their
forefathers was delivered up to the most wicked of the
heathen—first to the Romans, then to the Saracens, and
at last to the barbarous Turks.[8]

Finally, Danforth implies a direct equation between
the kingdom of God and the New England garden, ob-
serving that although God took down the partition between Jews and Gentiles and thus made the vine of the
church "spread its branches over the wall" there is "still
a distinction to be made . . . between a religious people
by a visible profession and the rest of the world that are
perishing for want of vision." God yet deals with "some
particular nations and people . . . in taking them to be
a select people to himself, in forming them to be a people peculiarly for himself to show forth his praise, by
erecting his visible kingdom in all the privileges, ordi-
nances, and worship thereof among them." And the
preacher asks, "Are we willing that God's mystical paradise, his garden of pleasure upon earth, should be quite
defaced, razed, and extinguish'd?" [9]

By the time Danforth the son was propounding this
question in 1714, the image of New England as God's
pleasure garden was being thoroughly subjected to the
pressures of modern history within the New England
microcosm. The rise of commerce and manufacturing,
of "rational and moral religion," and of an anticolonial
radicalism in politics evidenced the decisive rise of a
secular and modern New England in contrast to the
theocratic New England of the Puritans. Under this condition it would be expected that the authority of the
convenanted garden enclosed against the wilderness
would have lost its hold on the mind; that it would
become another lost American garden, passing into the

general realm of nostalgia for a lost pastoral age which the American imagination early began to create as a sentimental refuge from modernity. In fact, A. M. Plumstead lends his authority to the view that this did indeed occur. The attitude which the immediate and near descendants of the Puritan fathers took toward "the ideal days of the original errand," Plumstead says, relates them to that "little symbolic fable of America," the legend of Rip Van Winkle. Discovering themselves in a world "grown old much too fast," the New England ministers appear as "early versions of Rip Van Winkle, trying to rub the strangeness from their eyes as if they had suddenly returned to a society which had left them behind and was full of new ways and strange gods." [10] But, attractive as this suggestion is, is it appropriate to bring a Puritan minister like, say, the second Samuel Danforth into the realm of the Rip Van Winkle fable? Danforth lived in a dramatic state of anxiety over New England's apostasy, not to its literal past, but, as Increase Mather put it, to the "substance of that good old way." Basically, this meant the *presence* of God in New England. "The presence of God," Cotton Mather declares in his Election sermon of 1689, "this is no less than the very soul of New England; we are dead and gone if that withdraw." [11] The departure of God from New England, the utter spiritual deprivation of the garden leaving it again a waste and howling wilderness: this was the dread consequence of apostasy to the New England mission. It was not until the God of the Mathers and Danforths did substantially withdraw from New England that an Irvingesque nostalgia can be said to have become a motive in New England's literary attitude toward the past. We see this at work in Longfellow, Holmes, Lowell, and Whittier. But it is a qualified motive, especially in the Puritan Quaker, Whittier, whose greatest poem *Snow-Bound* transcends sentiment and nostalgia in Whittier's implied effort to discern the psychological and moral complexity of the New England garden.[12]

I am, I realize, no more than hinting at what I mean; and further I realize that what I am hinting at cannot be developed in the space available here. My intention is merely to indicate that if we can define a nostalgic mode of pastoral in New England, we can also define a more powerful apostatic mode. This is a mode which emerges in the mood of spiritual urgency that is conveyed in the pastoral images of posttheocratic New England. We may include among these, I suppose, the image of Jonathan Edwards in the woods outside the village of Northampton in 1737. Committed to his mission to restore an apostasized New England to its former state of purity by a repurification of the Puritan faith, Edwards lies "in the dust . . . emptied and annihilated . . . full of Christ alone . . . perfectly sanctified and made pure, with a divine and heavenly purity." [13] We may include the formidable image of Timothy Dwight in the next generation warning against "modern instances of declension" in the New England garden. By the time we come to Dwight, however, the convenanted garden is in a stage of significant metamorphosis. In Dwight the image of the gardener in the garden as the man of God, the minister, in reaction against modernity, merges with that of the man of letters confronting modernity. Dwight combines the functions of poet and preacher, or more broadly, of religion and literature; in poems like *Greenfield Hill* and *The Triumph of Infidelity,* he becomes a transitional figure in the New England garden—herald, although not by his conscious design, of a shift in the concept of this garden. No longer will it exist in the New England imagination under a religious covenant but more nearly, if more loosely, under a literary one.

In a panoramic series of pastoral images of New England we may include, and most significantly, the whole complex image of the garden of the New England Transcendentalists, our chief focus being on the village of Concord: Ralph Waldo Emerson in his "pleached garden"; Henry David Thoreau beside the waters of Walden Pond. We may include, too, the image of Hawthorne in the Concord garden—Hawthorne whose ironic version of the seventeenth-century New England in *The Scarlet Letter* subtly and fully comprehends the metaphor of New England as the enclosed garden of the covenant. We may include, too, the image of Emily Dickinson playing hide-and-seek with the Lord God of Hosts amid the flowers and shrubs of the Dickinson garden in Amherst, while across the street the church bell pealed and tolled a spinster's years away. We may include, too, the slightly later image of Henry Adams—Adams seeking for the power that was God in the cathedrals which dominate the pastoral fields of Normandy and discovering in his quest that "New England at its highest ideal power" is "beatified and glorified, in the Cathedral at Coutances." [14] We may include, too, the image of Robert Frost playing his own game of hide-and-seek with God in the pastures and woods of New Hampshire and Vermont. We may, in some distant and final sense, include too Robert Lowell meditating on the surprising conversions in Northampton in the 1730s or meditating upon the meaning of New England before Saint-Gaudens's bronze relief in memory of James Gould Shaw and his Negro regiment. Facing the Massachusetts State House on Beacon Street, the Shaw memorial (graphically appealed to in "For the Union Dead," 1959) is just above the Boston Public Garden, where (as described in Lowell's "The Public Garden," 1964) children out of school at five o'clock come in the lateness of an autumn after-

chosen by the finger of God, to possess it." [16] The initial Virginians, in other words, believed they had a covenant with God, and when they considered their failures, they saw these in the light of their failures in keeping this agreement.

But the assertion of a Virginia covenant against the forces of modern history was an impulse which lasted only momentarily in contrast to the duration of the New England religious thrust. By 1624 the Virginia Company had been, so to speak, expelled from the garden of Virginia by modern history. It had been dissolved by the King, an action Miller sees as resulting not from a conflict between the liberalism of George Sandys and an authoritarian ruler but from a vexatious triumph of pragmatic and materialistic modernity over the religious impulse. The "glorious mission" of Virginia to become a self-subsistent "holy edifice" erected in the wilderness to propagate the Gospel failed because the planters found no attraction to any crop except tobacco. Commenting "On Plantations" Francis Bacon had said that it would be wise to have less speculation about God's will for a new plantation and more information about what its soil would raise; in other words, the time had come when the vision of a colony in relation to an expanding imperial market of the nation-state would make outmoded visions of chosen people on errands to establish pleasure gardens of God in remote wildernesses. Thus before the Massachusetts Puritans had even embarked upon their errand into the wilderness, the people of Virginia had, Miller observes, "already gone through the cycle of exploration, religious dedication, disillusionment, and then reconciliation to a world in which making a living was the ultimate reality." An envisioned holy commonwealth of Virginia had been dispossessed by the new world centered in "commerce and reason." Virginia

had started on the road leading "from theology to com-
petition and expedience, where the decisive factor would
be, not the example of the Apostles, but the price per
pound of tobacco." [17]

But if this was so, yet it was hardly so. Paradoxically
the moment Virginia entered into modernity was also
the moment when Virginia began to evolve into a
uniquely reactionary community. It would eventually,
together with the other Southern colonies to be established, enter into a compact to share with the Northern
colonies emancipated from England by the Revolution
a federal government. But by this time Virginia and the
other Southern states were beginning to offer a strong
resistance to modernity, imagining themselves—idealiz-
ing themselves—as a providential and chosen community
struggling against dispossession by modern history.
Shortly this community would be destroyed as apostate
to modern history. In part—probably in considerable
part—this destruction would be owing to the apostatic
imagination of New England, the concentrated, most in-
tense and furious expression of this imagination stem-
ming from its power to summon back the Lord God of
Hosts as the leader of a mission to purify the American
garden of chattel slavery. When New Englanders called
upon that good brahminical matron-poetess of Boston,
Julia Ward Howe, to invoke His presence, she rose from
her bed early one morning, seized an old stump of a pen,
and wrote the invocation to battle: "Mine eyes have seen
the glory of the coming of the Lord, / He is trampling
out his vintage where the grapes of wrath are stored."

By the time this powerful summons to violence and
blood was written, Virginians, and Southerners as a
whole, had developed their own special sense of apostasy, having found abolitionist New England apostate to
the American Republic, to Christianity, and to civilization.

But let us return to the Virginia Company in the first age of colonialization. Deprived of the conception of Virginia as a covenant with God—of the covenant sensibility—how did the early Virginians imagine their destiny? The answer lies partially, I believe, in a necessary qualification of Miller's dramatic argument. Characteristically Miller overstates his case, placing a too literal emphasis on the language and terminology of certain spokesmen and failing to take completely into account that they are justifying a novel imperial venture in the name of old motives. The first settlement of Virginia represented more precisely the dissolution of the old religious community than its perpetuation. That this is so is attested to, I think, by the failure of the presence of God in Virginia. The God of the Virginia Company, or the God of its propagandists, did disappear—for, at any rate, a century or more. Apostasy to the spiritual mission of a former generation did not become a formative cultural motive in Virginia. The Virginians of the post–Virginia Company era made a different kind of response to modern history from that of the New Englanders, defining their mission not as an errand into a howling wilderness, in the midst of which as God's regenerate band they would make a pleasure garden for Him, but as an errand into an open, prelapsarian, self-yielding paradise, where they would be made regenerate by entering into a redemptive relationship with a new and abounding earth. The vision of Virginia as a paradise, in contrast to a wilderness, as a matter of fact, appears in the literature of the Virginia Company days, notably in the writings of Captain John Smith. But the appearance of such a vision in a developed form does not occur until nearly a century later, when it becomes a major aspect of Robert Beverley's remarkable work, *The History and Present State of Virginia.*

Published in London in 1705, this book offers an ecstatic and sensuous vision of the paradisical garden of Virginia. All of the second part—"Of the NATURAL *Product and Conveniencies* of VIRGINIA; In ITS Unimprov'd STATE, before the *English* went thither"—is virtually a fertility hymn in praise of Virginia's waters and fish, and of its soils, native fruits, herbs, and grains. When Beverley comes to consider "the Husbandry and Improvements of the Country"—that is, the development of the Virginian plantations—he is also at times in a near ecstasy. Tending not so much to juxtapose as to blend the delights of the natural garden and the plantation garden, he finds a memorable symbol in the summer house of Colonel William Byrd I:

> Have you pleasures in a Garden? All things thrive in it, most surpriseingly [sic]; you can't walk by a Bed of Flowers, but besides the entertainment of their Beauty, your Eyes will be saluted with the charming colours of the Humming Bird, which revels among the Flowers, and licks off the Dew and Honey from their tender Leaves, on which it only feeds. It's size is not half so large as an *English* Wren, and its colour is a glorious shining mixture of Scarlet, Green, and Gold. Colonel Byrd, in his Garden, which is the finest in that Country, has a Summer-House set round with the *Indian* Honey-Suckle, which all the summer is continually full of sweet Flowers, in which these Birds delight exceedingly. Upon these Flowers, I have seen ten or a dozen of these beautiful Creatures together, which sported about me so familiarly, that with their little Wings they often fann'd my Face.[18]

In his desire to make a complete harmony of Virginia as a natural and an improved garden—"a paradise improved"—Beverley offers a poetic evocation of a plantation summer house and almost ignores the concrete details of the life on the plantation. But in Beverley's poetic evocation we have the origin of the plantation in the literary imagination as the fruition of the errand into paradise. The glimpse of a planter like a Beverley or a Byrd seated pleasantly amid the honeysuckle and the hummingbirds in that faraway summer, foreshadows the evocation in literary imagining of a pastoral plantation situated in a timeless "Old South," a secure world redeemed from the ravages of history, a place of pastoral independence and pastoral permanence. To the incomplete scene we have only to add the plantation mansion and the planter, who has in hand a well-worn copy of Virgil, and within a supervisory distance a group of Negro slaves amiably at work in a tobacco field.

At the time Beverley wrote his "honest Account of the ancientest, as well as the most profitable Colony, depending on the Crown of *England*," [19] the significance of the individual plantation as a symbol of independent dominion had only begun to emerge. The translation of paradise into the "paradise improved" desired by Beverley occurs specifically in the imagination of William Byrd II, or as he is best known, William Bryd of Westover. It can, in fact, be documented in one letter Byrd wrote in 1726 to an old acquaintance, the Earl of Orrery. Byrd, lately returned from what proved to be his last journey to the mother country, explains the benefits of life in Virginia, if with a poignant reservation:

> Besides the advantage of a pure air, we abound in all kinds of provisions without expense (I mean we who have plantations). I have a large family of my own, and my doors are open to everybody, yet I have no bills to pay, and half-a-crown will rest undisturbed in my pockets for many moons together. Like one of the patriarchs, I have my flock and herds, my bondmen and bondwomen, and every sort of trade amongst my own servants, so that I live in a kind of independence on everyone but Providence. However, though this sort of life is without ex-

pense, yet it is attended with a great deal of trouble. I
must take care to keep all my people to their duty, to set
all the springs in motion, and to make everyone draw his
equal share to carry the machine forward. But then 'tis
an amusement in this silent country and a continual exer-
cise of our patience and economy. Another thing, My
Lord, that recommends this country very much: we sit
securely under our vines and our fig trees without any
danger to our property. We have neither public robbers
nor private, which your Lordship will think very strange
when we have often needy governors and pilfering con-
victs sent amongst us. . . . Thus, My Lord we are very
happy in our Canaans if we could but forget the onions
and fleshpots of Egypt.[20]

In William Byrd's letter to Lord Orrery, we note, the
fulfillment of the errand into paradise is realized exclu-
sively in terms of the plantation society of Virginia. This
society, if in ironic playfulness, is identified with the
promised land of the archetypal Exodus: the plantations
of Virginia are New Canaans, which are a powerful and
complete salvation from a land in which the allurements
of evil have been a bondage. But the most significant
feature of Byrd's vision is that it identifies the new way
of life gained by the errand into paradise with the plantation master's supervision of "bondmen and bond-
women." He may refer both to indentured servants and
to slaves; but we can assume Byrd refers mostly to his
increasing force of chattel slaves. Such an assumption is
supported by the preoccupation with slavery that is
found elsewhere in his letters and in other writings during the last third of Byrd's career. This was the age of
a rapid growth in the number of slaves imported into
Virginia in answer to the increasing need for cheap labor
in the production of tobacco which could be priced low
enough to compete effectively in the European markets.

The large importation of slaves was not a considered act. It was an expediency brought about by unpredictable changes in an international market.

In evaluating the result of this, and perhaps without necessarily indicating approval of other general theses of his noted book on slavery in America, I can appeal to the authority of Stanley Elkins. He makes, I think, a most telling point about the introduction of African chattel slavery into the colonial South:

> There was nothing "natural" about it; it had no necessary connection with either tropical climate or tropical crops: in Virginia and Maryland, where the institution first appeared and flourished, the climate was hardly tropical, and the staple crop—tobacco—might have been grown as far north as Canada. It had nothing to do with characteristics which might have made the Negro peculiarly suited either to slavery or the labor of tobacco culture. Slavery in past ages had been limited to no particular race, and the earliest planters of colonial Virginia appear to have preferred a laboring force of white servants from England, Scotland, and Ireland, rather than of blacks from Africa. Nor was it a matter of common-law precedent, for the British colonists who settled in areas eventually to be included in the United States brought with them no legal categories comparable to that of "slave," as the term would be understood by the end of the seventeenth century. "Slavery," considered in the abstract as servile bondage, had existed elsewhere for centuries; indeed, the native of Africa had known it intimately. Yet nothing was inherent, even in the fact of *Negro* slavery, which should compel it to take the form that it took in North America. Negro slavery flourished in Latin America at that same period, but there the system was strikingly different. In certain altogether crucial respects slavery as we know it was not imported from elsewhere but was created in America—fashioned on the

spot by Englishmen in whose traditions such an institution had no part. American slavery was unique, in the
sense that, for symmetry and precision of outline, nothing like it had ever previously been seen.

When the colonial Virginians expedientially committed themselves—and the South—to African slavery, they
instigated an opposition to modern history that they
could not institutionalize within the framework of their
civilizational tradition. Out of expediency, in other
words, they bound themselves to an action that in effect
transcended reaction, for it transcended the continuity
of their history. But they of course did not realize this.
The imagination always works to accommodate novelty
to received patterns. With its eruption into the colonial
South, beginning in the third decade of the eighteenth
century, chattel slavery asked to be taken into the general
myth of the New World as a reactionary and redemptive
garden; or, more specifically speaking, it demanded to
be incorporated in the myth of the South as an errand
into paradise. We can see the process commencing in
Byrd's letter to Orrery. At this stage it seems to be com-
paratively simple and painless, involving no more than
the creation—out of a stock of images familiar to the
colonial mind—of an image of the slave society as a patriarchal garden. But as the population of "Ethiopians"
continued to increase, Byrd became conscious of the
difficulty of assuming the assimilation of slavery to the
pastoral ideal. Slaves, he said in a letter to the Earl of
Egmont in 1736, "blow up the pride and ruin the industry of our white people, who, seeing a rank of poor
creatures below them, detest work for fear it should
make them look like slaves. Then that poverty, which will
ever attend upon idleness, disposes them as much to
pilfer as it does the Portuguese, who account it much more
like a gentleman to steal than to dirty their hands with

labor of any kind." Byrd feared too that masters faced with large numbers of slaves would be required to ride them with "a taut rein." This necessity could be "terrible to a good-natured man, who must submit to be either a fool or a fury." The most fearful prospect Byrd envisioned was a servile war instituted by the "descendants of Ham" under the leadership of some "man of desperate courage." This possibility moved him to think that the British Parliament ought to consider the abolition of slavery, or at least a ban on the further importation of black chattels into the colonies.[22] Such promptings of fear did not become overriding considerations with Byrd. He belonged to a world in which slavery had become a necessity—a world in which necessity would be more and more equated with historical destiny. Accepting the developing actuality of his society—the centrality of chattel slavery in his world—Byrd continued to explore the image of the patriarchical garden. His most significant evocation of it, besides the letter to Orrery, may well be a letter ten years later to Peter Beckford of Jamaica. Byrd was interested in having Beckford, a man of great wealth, as a visitor at Westover, probably hoping to sell him land.

I had the honor to pay you my Respects in June last & to send you as perfect a description of my seat of Westover as truth would permit me. I represented it honestly as it is & us'd not the french liberty of dressing it up as it ought to be. But since my last I have got a person to make a draught of it which perhaps will appear a little rough, but if it should not be found according to Art, it will make amends by being according to truth. Many particulars are left out which could not conveniently be crowded in to so small a Plan, but the Garden & chief of the Buildings are comprehended. I wish all my Heart it may tempt you at least to make us a visit in the Spring

in order to see it. But if the Torrid Zone be still your
choice & you should resolve to lay your Bones where you
first drew your Breath, be so good as to honour this
Country with one of your sons, of which I hear you are
blest with several, you may make a Prince of Him for less
money here than you can make Him a Private Gentleman
in England. We live here in Health & in Plenty, in In-
nocense & Security, fearing no Enemy from Abroad or
Robbers at home. Our Government too, is so happily
constituted that a Governour must first outwit us before
he can oppress us, and if ever he squeeze money out of
us he must first take care to deserve it. Our negroes are
not so numerous or so enterprizeing as to give us any
apprehension or uneasiness nor indeed is their Labour
any other than Gardening & less by far that what the poor
People undergo in other countrys. Nor are any crueltys
exercized upon them, unless by great accident they happen to fall into the hands of a Brute, who always passes
here for a monster. We all lye securely with our Doors
unbarred & can travel the whole country without either
arms or Guard, and all this not for want of money or
Rogues, but because we have no great citys to shelter the
Thief or Pawn-Brokers to receive what he steals.[23]

The most interesting aspect of Byrd's letter to Beckford is the definition of the role of the chattel slave in
the idealized plantation garden. The blacks are not numerous (when in fact their numbers were steadily increasing). Save for gross exception, they are never
treated harshly. They are the gardeners in the garden.
If Byrd's recognition that in the imagination of the plantation garden the slave, not the master, must be ac-
corded the figurative role of the gardener appears to be
hardly more than incidental, it is one of his most important meanings in the literary history of the South. Byrd
defined poetically an anxiety that was beginning to haunt
the Virginia masters. It was an anxiety about laborers in

the earth that was not present in countries where the "poor people" toiled on the land in their role as a peasantry. It was not necessary to think of these people; they did not truly exist except as a part of the immemorial landscape. They were part and parcel of the lord's possession, both actually and imaginatively, of the land. But chattel slaves were property in themselves. The lord of a chattel slave had property in land and property in the slave. The two possessions were not identical but separate. Not only did the master know this but the slave knew it. Thus arose a fear compounded by the racial dimension of slavery but not produced by it: the fear of slavery as being not simply a threat to the social order but of its being a subversion of the very source of order—that is, the mind and imagination.

For subtly attached to the metaphor of the plantation as a pastoral social order, in which the chattel is the gardener, is a more complex metaphorical notion—one that derives primarily from the Western (and not the Hebraic) pastoral. This is the idea of the plantation as a homeland of the life of the mind. In the letter to Lord Orrery, Byrd's vision of the plantation as a pastoral community fundamentally derives from the Virgilian imagination of a pastoral world which is a symbolic place of the literary mind and spirit. In the *Eclogues* Virgil established Arcadia in the literary imagination as a dominion of the life of the literary mind. Arcadia, together with the urban image of the mind (and often in contrast to it) became a primary symbol of literary community in the Renaissance, presenting the image of the philosopher and/or the poet—i.e., the man of letters—in rural retirement, living autonomously in the mind, and yet in an isolation meaningful only because it is in relation to the community of men of letters and learning. The library in the garden—e.g., Pope's grotto at Twickenham—is a pastoral image supporting the concept of the independent, secular, eighteenth-century mind following the pursuits of literature and knowledge. Byrd among his thirty-six hundred books at Westover, engaged in his correspondence with other men of letters, is a figure in the community of the eighteenth-century mind. The pastoral pose may seem superficial in Byrd, as in a letter to John Boyle in 1726: "We that are banished from these polite pleasures [in London] are forced to take up with rural entertainment. A library, a garden, a grove, and a purling stream are the innocent scenes that divert our leisure." [24] But in the context of the adaptation of the pastoral convention in America, William Byrd of Westover is the first full-fledged embodiment of a singular figure in American and, you might say, in Western literature: the patriarch-philosophe—the slave master and man of letters—of the Southern plantation world. He forecasts a greater and more intricate embodiment of this figure in Thomas Jefferson of Monticello.

When we move from the age of Byrd to that of Jefferson, we come into a slaveholders' world which Byrd anticipates, yet which is a more various and complex world than Byrd's imagination encountered. Comparing Monticello to Westover, we may in a sense think of Monticello as a symbol of modernity, associating it not with any reaction to modern history but primarily with the emancipation of the humanistic mind of the Enlightenment. It is true that what Jefferson, and the Enlightenment, prized above all—independence of the humanistic mind—is not what modern history has necessarily prized. It would seem that insofar as the Enlightenment emancipated the mind of Western humanism—completing a process begun in late medieval times—it liberated a power more often hostile to the forces of change than favorable to them. The discontent of an emancipated humanism with modernity would not become obvious, however, until the entire emergence of industrialism, nationalism, and democracy in the nineteenth century. When in the later eighteenth century—in the full tide of the American Enlightenment—Jefferson conceived and, with slave labor, built the perfection of plantations on his little mountain outside Charlottesville, Virginia, he was consciously creating a major American symbol of the rise of the secular mind. The garden of Monticello—the mansion and its environs as conceived in Jefferson's highly educated, and poetic, imagination, an imagination informed with the poetry of knowledge—came into existence as a symbol of the cosmopolitan dominion of the Enlightenment mind. It was a center of the Republic of Letters, bearing a relation to Philadelphia, as Pope's Twickenham bore a relation to London, but at the same time having a broader relation to London, Paris, or St. Petersburg. Like Voltaire's estate at Ferney, it existed in a tension between the urban and the pastoral domains of letters, a symbolic tension at once antagonistic and complementary; and one far more complex than that between Virgil's Rome and Virgil's Arcadia. Monticello was the most exquisite American expression of the eighteenth-century redemption of the mind from the "ages of superstition" by the faith in reason and knowledge. Jefferson's plantation—where the mind existed in a setting of pastoral permanence—represented the Enlightenment idealization of a capacity for detachment, for the transcendent contemplation of man and society and the world. Monticello was a symbol of the independence of mind that the eighteenth century associated, in Jean Paul Sartre's words, with "the permanent power for forming and criticizing ideas." [25]

But this garden of the mind had not only been made by slave labor, it had been made to function as the center of a large agricultural enterprise carried on by chattels and their overseers. Jefferson, for all his opposition to slavery—he once declared that one hour of slavery was worse than ages of British oppression—actively participated all of his life in the ever-expanding world the slaveholders were making in America. Owner of around two hundred slaves, he bought and sold slaves and hunted down his runaways. He wrote a slave code for Virginia and opposed any limitation on the expansion of slavery in the nation. He emancipated only two slaves in his lifetime, and one of these bought his freedom. It can be said, as a matter of fact, that Jefferson's support of the slave system in a pragmatic sense was as sound as any Virginian's. He was, to be sure, locked into the pragmatics of slavery by his need to support his often precarious hold on his ten thousand acres of land by the value of his chattels. Thus for over fifty years Jefferson was devoted not only to the economy of slave labor but to the economy of property in slaves themselves.[26] About six years before his death Jefferson wrote to his manager about the treatment of slaves by the overseers:

> I have had no reason to believe that any overseer, since Griffin's time has over worked them. accordingly, the deaths among the grown ones seem ascribable to natural causes, but the loss of 5. little ones in 4 years induces me to fear that the overseers do not permit the women to devote as much time as is necessary to the care of their children: that they view their labor as the 1st object and the raising their child but as secondary. I consider the labor of a breeding woman as no object, and that a child raised every 2. years is of more profit than the crop of the best laboring man. in this, as in all other cases, providence has made our interests and our duties coincide perfectly. . . . I must pray to inculcate upon the over-

seers that it is not their [the slaves'] labor, but their increase which is the first consideration with us.[27]

In the garden of Monticello lurked a beast; one that had appeared in dim outline in the garden of Westover. Now it was a sinister shadow in the foliage: the question of the relationship of chattel slavery to mind. How many times and with what varying degrees of ferocity the beast may have sprung on Thomas Jefferson is, I suppose, a matter about which we may conjecture. The most memorable record Jefferson left of its presence in the garden is in his famous *Notes on the State of Virginia,* the work on which Jefferson's contemporary reputation as a philosopher chiefly rested. Not quite a direct record, it is all the more dramatic for not being so. The record is to be found first in Jefferson's argument concerning the natural inferiority of the African and the necessity of colonizing emancipated slaves in order to prevent a degradation of both the bodily and intellectual endowments of the white race. In this argument (Query xiv, on law and the administration of justice), Jefferson is the philosophe, calm and detached, pointing with what he considered to be scientific certainty to the inferior status of Negroes in the Chain of Being and yet arguing for the emancipation of an acknowledged part of the human species as a necessity of moral law and order.[28] But Jefferson's rational control of the problem of slavery breaks down, and in the eighteenth query of the *Notes on Virginia* we get his most noted denunciation of the institution. The importance of the eighteenth query springs not so much from slavery as a political or an economic issue or—as we use the term today—a "social" issue. It comes from the fact that in Jefferson's view it is fundamentally a problem in "manners." *"The particular customs and manners that may happen to be received in that State?"* This is the query

to which Jefferson addresses himself, and he does so with
the full consciousness of the eighteenth-century educated sensibility, which was attuned, as no century had
been before, to the meaning of "customs and manners."
The critical intelligence of this century, intensely concerned with finding the standards of civilization, conceived manners to be the very deportment of civility.
Thus Jefferson opens his response to the query with a
generalization of the problem that was central in the
discussion: "It is difficult to determine on the standard
by which the manners of a nation may be tried, whether
*catholic* or *particular*. It is more difficult for a native to
bring to that standard the manners of his own nation,
familiarized to him by habit." This is as far as Jefferson
proceeds with rational generalizations on the query. He
seizes immediately upon what might appear to be only
one aspect of an inquiry into the manners of Virginians:
the influence of slavery on the manners of "our people,"
by whom it turns out he means those of the master class.
Jefferson does not admit of other possible influences,
nor does he admit of the possibility of this influence
being mixed in character. Declaring it to be "doubtless
an unhappy influence," he launches into a far more drastic criticism of slavery than anything William Byrd had
said earlier. Jefferson totally condemns slavery as a corruption of civility so fundamental it precludes even the
possibility of an education in civility. Both within the
family and within the state the existence of slavery provides for an irresistible education in tyranny: "The whole
commerce between master and slave is a perpetual exer-
cise of the most boisterous passions, the most unremit-
ting despotism on the one part, and degrading submis-
sion on the other." Slavery also provides for an irresistible
attraction to indolence: "With the morals of the people,
their industry . . . is destroyed. For in a warm climate,

no man will labour for himself who can make another labour for him. This is so true, that of the proprietors of slaves a very small proportion indeed are ever seen to labour." Finally, the unhappy influence of slavery makes for a fatal alienation, a separation of the masters from the ultimate origin of liberty as the gift of God. God will not suffer this violation of His power: "Indeed I tremble for my country when I reflect that God is just: that his justice cannot sleep forever: that considering numbers, nature and natural means only, a revolution of the wheel of fortune, is among possible events: that it may become probable by supernatural interference!" The concluding portion of the eighteenth query, with its forecast of a servile revolt instigated directly by God, is the most astounding part of it. The appeal which Jefferson makes here is not to "Nature's God," the serene Deity of the Declaration of Independence. In considering slavery as an unhappy influence on manners, Jefferson comes close to making the God of liberty into a Lord God of Hosts who is jealous of his gifts and terrible in his justice upon those who in pride and greed misuse them or deny them. In the eighteenth query the only hope Jefferson sees is that the God of liberty present in the American Revolution will not withdraw His presence from the garden but that "under the auspices of heaven" the Revolution is operating to produce "a total emancipation" of the slaves "with the consent of the masters, rather than by their extirpation." [29]

In spite of the note of hope, Jefferson's vision in the eighteenth query is hardly less than one of the utter confounding of the errand into paradise. It is almost a prophecy—a revelation—of the ironic end of the errand in the wasting of the Southern New Canaan by a God whose wrath is like that of the Puritan God.

But what most deeply informs Jefferson's apocalyptic

vision of slavery is not some deviation on Jefferson's part into a Calvinistic state of guilt about the treatment of slaves. Jefferson was not concerned about the influence of slavery on the slaves but with its influence on the minds of the slave holders. A response to a query about the manners of the community, his singular vision of the evils of slavery—a refinement and intensification of Byrd's insight into these evils—conveys the idea not only of outward deportment but of inner discipline; Jefferson is concerned with the influence of the role of slavery on the education of the mind. Central to Jefferson's vision of society, this concern is basic in *Notes on Virginia.* The book exemplifies the application of the critical mind to the condition of life in Virginia and its prospects, being a set of rational discussions of a set of queries propounded to Jefferson by a fellow philosophe. The *Notes* demonstrate the function of mind in Sartre's conception of the eighteenth-century critical mind. In contemplating slavery Jefferson discovers the subversion of this function. Slavery not only corrupts the young mind with the passion of command, it not only severs the connection between the mind of the master class and the soil, but it defies the very scrutiny of mind. Slavery destroys the very capacity for rational criticism. It implies the drastic dispossession of the pastoral vision of the plantation as a dominion of mind.

Jefferson seems never again to have come so close to discovering the implication of the association between mind and plantation. No doubt he had come close enough, which may be one reason why in the query immediately following that on manners and customs (that is, Query xix) Jefferson turns an argument against manufacturing in America into a poetic vision of the American redemption of civilization from a Europe corrupted by cities and factories. "Those who labour in the earth are the chosen people of God, if ever he had a chosen people, whose breasts he has made his peculiar deposit for substantial and genuine virtue," Jefferson proclaims.[30] And in language charged with scriptural and apocalyptic intensity he not only repudiates a corrupt Europe but by distinct implication repudiates the corrupt world of the American slaveholders. In this vision—an apocalypse counter to the apocalypse of slavery—in which he describes the heart of the yeoman farmer as the place of God's "peculiar deposit" of true virtue, Jefferson in effect sets forth the small self-subsistent farm rather than the slave plantation as properly the peculiar institution of America. The vision of the yeoman farmer represents not only a pastoral purification of European influences but of the influence of slavery. The independent farmer is identified as the—and, we may say, the sole—figure in the American landscape and his freehold as the symbolic dominion of the mind.

Probably we can define in Jefferson's mind a vision which mediated or reconciled the grim apocalypse of the slavery plantation and the shining apocalypse of the yeoman farm. This is a vision in which the plantation is transformed into the image resembling the Roman villa idealized as a dominion of the independent mind by Cicero in the *Tusculan Disputations* or by Horace in one of the *Epodes:*

> Happy is he who far from business,
> like the first race of man,
> can till inherited lands with his teams,
> free from all payment of interest.
>
> He who avoids the market and
> the proud thresholds of mighty citizens. . . .

Jefferson, retiring to Monticello from the presidency, wrote in 1810:

My mornings are devoted to correspondence. From breakfast to dinner, I am in my shops, my garden, or on horseback among my farms; from dinner to dark, I give to society and recreation with my neighbors and friends; and from candle light to early-bed, I read.—My health is perfect, and my strength considerably reinforced by the activity of the course I pursue. . . . I talk of ploughs and harrows, of seeding and harvesting, with my neighbors, and of politics, too . . . and feel, at length, the blessing of being free to say and do what I please, without being responsible for it to any mortal. A part of my occupation, by no means the least pleasing, is the direction of the studies of such young men as ask it . . . I endeavor to keep their attention fixed on the main objects of all science, the freedom and happiness of man.[31]

In this vision Monticello is a patrician domain of the mind over which African chattel slavery has no influence because it is simply excluded. Slaves, like the peasants of European pastoral, are presumably about the plantations; but they are its unobtrusive gardeners.

But Jefferson himself may well have known that both his apocalyptic vision of the yeoman dominion and his quieter vision of the plantation as Roman villa were evocations of pastoral nostalgia—idealizations of or appeals to Virginia's continuity with cultural situations that never really existed. They were appeals to the errand into paradise—or more nearly to the rationale of the errand: the pastoral purification of Europe. The actuality of Virginia and of the South that was coming into being Jefferson recognized in his vision of slavery and its center, the slave plantation. The mind belonged to the world the slaveholders—he himself one of them—were making. This was a world which the Southern imagination would unsuccessfully endeavor to represent in terms of a pastoral garden of the chattel, seeking to make a covenant between the literary mind and chattel slavery, to make slavery the condition of the independent mind. The attempt would inevitably fail, but in failing would subject the Southern literary mind to a process of alienation—a process which paradoxically would assure that one day the antebellum South's experience of alienation would rise to literary significance.

# TWO

# Slavery and the
# Culture of Alienation

"Let all your game lie in the constant recognition &
assertion of a Southern *nationality!*"
—William Gilmore Simms
to William Porcher Miles (1857)

I ASSUME I NEED NOT GO TO ANY LENGTH TO DOCUMENT
the existence of the culture of alienation. In a large sense
I mean by the term that special community of discontent
and disaffection formed by writers and artists in the general Western culture when, in the breaking apart of
Christendom and the rise of modern history, they began
to experience a deficiency of wholeness, or, we may say,
an incapacity to experience a cultural wholeness. We can
trace such an experience in the Western literary mind
and spirit from Petrarch to its first great expression in
Shakespeare and Cervantes. But the culture of alienation
did not begin to be entirely apprehended until the nineteenth century, following the failure of the Enlightenment dream of a restoration of wholeness to the general
culture by an all-encompassing rationalism. At this time
the motto of the culture of literary alienation was suc-
cinctly formulated by Baudelaire: "The man of letters is
the world's enemy." And although Baudelaire was ex-
pressing a sentiment that perhaps has a more precise

meaning in the context of the opposition of French writers to the French bourgeois, his declaration has a broad and fundamental signification in the literary history of the nineteenth and twentieth centuries.[1] It declares what seems to become a necessary attitude on the part of the writer following the decline of the eighteenth-century world. If in the eighteenth-century world the emancipation of the literary mind—of mind in general—had seemed assured because intellect and letters had become one of the orders of existence, the assurance was vitiated by the rapid acceleration of modernity in the first half of the following century. Finance capitalism, industrialism, the technology of machines, the expansion of theoretical science, the insurgence of radical democracy—all of these forces threatened any kind of order which assumed the validity of the literary mind, rooted as it was in the classical-Christian—the humanistic—tradition. An estrangement of the humanistic mind began to appear to be the condition not only of its freedom but of its survival.

As the humanistic reaction to modernity became more desperate, it gave rise to complex and contradictory attitudes. But its motivation remained independence of mind—the motive that had accounted for the rise of mind embodied in the eighteenth-century man of letters as philosophe. In a sense the alienation of the literary consciousness in the nineteenth century was a further stage of the eighteenth-century emancipation of the critical faculty of mind.

The culture of alienation is not as clearly defined in the sparse literary history of the nineteenth-century United States as it is in the massive literary history of contemporary Europe. But basically it is a continuation of what I have referred to as the pastoral reaction to modernity in the America of colonial and early national times—a reaction which occurred under the novel conditions of American existence—conditions that were ironically more compelling in the South than in New England. From the beginning of the American Republic—which assumed as its quasi-official image the emergence of a new nation in a New World, an image opposing the decadence of an Old World—the South was the most novel part of the novel nation in history. It was a chattel slave society without historical reference in the Anglo-Saxon civilization from which its religion, law, and letters descended; and as a matter of fact it was without any very credible parallels in the contemporary slave societies. The imperative quest of the South was for a basis on which firmly to establish itself as a novel civilization. But the quest was so constricted by the pressure of historical expediency—by the South's need to defend its singular historical situation—that the quest had little time to develop philosophical amplitude and depth. A meditative or contemplative inquiry into the "truth" of the South was demanded, but there was no time for this. In New England the situation was quite different. The Puritans had brought to the New World a total way of life—based on a fully formulated world view. The expression of this view (which can be taken as one attempt to remedy the modern deficiency of wholeness) was entrusted to a body of learned clerics, who as time went on expanded into a group resembling what Coleridge called in England a "clerisy" and Oliver Wendell Holmes in New England referred to as "the academic races"—a body of ministers, lawyers, teachers, statesmen, civil servants—all, in the contemporary meaning of the term, men of letters. The New England clerisy was often divided by bitter quarreling, but over the years it adapted the New England way to historical changes and it assumed the responsibility for New England's role in the Republic,

albeit in its division over this role it created the Essex
Junto and the first secession movement within the infant
nation. The South at the beginning of the new nation was
certainly not without an intellectual class, but it was a
more loosely formulated one, lacking a unifying origin
in a historical mission. By the commencement of the
nineteenth century, the history of the South had evolved
out of diversity into a way of life that demanded the
formulation of a world view. This called urgently for the
creation of an intellectual elite in the South. Such a class
of men of letters did arise in the nineteenth-century
South, and it developed and expressed a Southern view
of the world. But by the time Southern men of letters
became aware of their existence as Southern men of
letters, the whole conception of the function of the man
of letters—not to say the very conception of the man of
letters and, more deeply, the very conception of lit-
eracy—was being put into question by the forces of modern history. The literary culture of the Western civilization was beginning to take on the definable aspect of the
culture of alienation.

I cannot here explore the Southern literary experience
in relation to the culture of alienation beyond suggestion. And I am somewhat painfully aware that I have
ventured on this suggestion in another place—so that I
may seem simply to be repeating myself. I wish, however,
to expand, and in a way to revise, my earlier remarks
pertaining to the subject at hand. These comments
(which appear in my essay entitled "The Southern
Writer and the Great Literary Secession" [2]) were to the
effect that the South's lack of distinguished literary ac-
complishment in the nineteenth century—save perhaps
for Poe's achievement which I emphasize was in considerable part related to his life outside the South—can be
attributed to its being cut off from the literary sensibility

of the larger world, the culture of alienation. I do not make the point in quite this way, but that is the import of what I attempt to say. The antebellum Southern writer, I say, was cut off from what affected the general stream of literary culture because of the involvement of the Southern man of letters in the politics of slavery. He could not participate in the opposition to society which distinguishes the function of the man of letters in Europe, and in New England, where it marks in important ways the writings of Emerson, Thoreau, and Hawthorne.

I observe, in other words, that in its politicalization the antebellum Southern literary mind did not undergo an experience of alienation from its own—the Southern —society; and lacking this experience failed to experience the reaction to modernity—the deep discontent with modern civilization—which informs and gives power to the modern writer. But I now think that I oversimplified the situation. A fuller evaluation of it requires us to recognize that the proslavery argument involved a frustrated effort of the Southern literary mind to participate in the culture of alienation; and that there may perhaps be defined an antebellum Southern version of the culture of alienation that is as significant in American literary history as the New England version. (This is not to say that the Southern version is equal in intrinsic literary achievement to the New England version.) In New England the pastoral reaction to modernity became an integral expression of the crisis of alienation and thus a fulfillment of the quest for independence of mind. The culture of alienation found a perfect manifestation in the hut Thoreau constructed with materials costing twenty-eight-dollars and twelve and one-half cents on Emerson's land in Walden Woods. Here Thoreau lived for a time—planting a bean patch and catching fish from

Walden Pond, a lone gardener in his garden. You are, his friend Ellery Channing told Thoreau, engaged in "the grand process of devouring yourself alive." [3] But Thoreau went to Walden Woods not to munch on his own soul in introverted isolation, but to oppose society's obsession with modernity. If the motives of his opposition were complex, they may be summed up as a desire to respiritualize the New England garden. Thoreau was a figure of the apostatic gardener in the New England garden of the literary covenant.

But in the South of the same age the pastoral reaction to modernity issued essentially in the progressive frustration of the pastoral mode of consciousness. As this may be traced in antebellum Southern men of letters, it involves a struggle to accommodate the pastoral mode to the antipastoral novelty of the South as expressed by the institution of African chattel slavery. This is not a simple struggle, and to describe it in exact analysis is probably impossible. Surely it is not a task for the present limited comment. I shall deal with it briefly and schematically.

Let us assume that in historical perspective we can see the struggle occurring in three overlapping stages. In each of these stages we see a continuing struggle in the Southern literary mind against accepting the meaning of the garden of the chattel—namely, that is, that the South constitutes a unique slave society. The struggle was never to be fully resolved. But it moves from a time when the Southern mind resists the identification with slavery to a time when the master-slave relationship is accepted as the proper symbol of the Southern mind: from a time when a Southern resistance to modernity is seen in terms of a pastoral alienation of the South to a time when this resistance is seen in terms of the isolation of a slave nation from modernity.

The first stage, as I have already suggested in the last lecture, is evident in Jefferson—in the conflict between an agrarianism which is a metaphor of intellectual and spiritual independence and a recognition of the Southern plantation as a symbol of the tyranny of slavery over the mind. But the conflict, although expressed intensely in the *Notes on the State of Virginia,* was one that Jefferson did not allow to become desperate. This was partly because he was able to take, or was forced to take, a pragmatic attitude toward slavery. It may have been more basically because he was willing on pragmatic grounds to compromise his devotion to the pastoral vision, allowing as time went on for its modification in the light of his recognition of the need for manufacturing in America. In a yet more fundamental—in an overall sense—it may have been because Jefferson did not feel an intractable opposition between the expansion of a slave society and the independence of mind. He continued to feel, with the detachment of the philosophe, that Monticello afforded a perspective from which the mind could view the world, not be separated from it. But in Jefferson's slightly younger contemporary, John Taylor of Caroline, we become aware of a desperate attitude toward the insurgency into the nineteenth-century society of democracy and capitalism—the society of "paper and patronage," as he dubbed it. Taylor saw an entirely false ethic coming into being; between it and the agrarian way there could be no compromise. In Taylor a pastoral purification of modernity reaches ultimate pietistic heights. Not only does he envision agriculture as the source of union of practical affairs and moral principles and thus the "best architect of a complete man," it is the only source of man's redemption. Taylor was drawn toward a pastoral eschatology:

Poetry, in allowing more virtue to agriculture, than any other profession, has abandoned her privilege of fiction, and yielded to the natural moral effect of the absence of temptation. The same fact is commemorated by religion, upon an occasion the most solemn, within the scope of human imagination. At the awful day of judgment, the discrimination of the good from the wicked, is not made by the criterion of sects or of dogmas, but by one which constitutes the daily employment and the great end of agriculture. The judge upon this occasion has by anticipation pronounced, that to feed the hungry, clothe the naked, and give drink to the thirsty, are the passports to future happiness; and the divine intelligence which selected an agricultural state as a paradise for its first favourites, has here again prescribed the agricultural virtues as the means for the admission of their posterity into heaven.[4]

Such an elevation of the theme of pastoral permanence represents a narrowing, deepening, and intensification of the feeling of agrarian frustration in the Southern mind. Far more than Jefferson, Taylor expresses a need to reconcile slavery to pastoral piety. For Taylor did not as did Jefferson have optional visions of the Southern destiny. He saw that slavery must be institutionalized in Southern agriculture. There was no other choice. Even though "Negro slavery is a misfortune to agriculture," Taylor says, "it is incapable of removal, and only within the reach of palliation." Taylor believed that palliation required among other things the suppression of "a race or nation of people between the masters and slaves, having rights extremely different from within, called free negroes and mulattoes." [5] To make the necessary dependence of agriculture on slavery as effective as possible, Taylor advocated the resettlement of all free

Negroes. His ultimate idea was that in reducing the bad effects of slavery on agriculture to a minimum Southerners could allow agriculture to perform its function of a total redemption of life. In the garden of the chattel the fully submissive slave would not so much unite the master to the land as be the least possible impediment to the union.

A further stage of complication in the Southern pastoral consciousness can be detected in John Randolph of Roanoke. Randolph was more opposed to slavery than Taylor. Under pressure of the initial phase of abolitionism, he became a reluctant defender of slavery—not because of its moral rightness but because he thought that the anarchic tendencies of abolitionists not only encouraged slave rebellions but threatened the whole fabric of social order. When he made a will in 1821 in which he freed his slaves, providing them upon his death with lands he owned in Ohio, Randolph hoped that his gesture would help cure what he called "a cancer" on the face of his beloved Virginia.[6] It was a gesture in the direction of gradual emancipation. And yet Randolph did not feel that slavery was an entire evil. In the retrospective vision that more and more gripped his mind, he conceived that once in a simpler and more virtuous age it had been allied to a gentry who had something like the harmonious pastoral companionship with slaves we glimpse as an ideal in John Taylor. The masters redeemed their property in men by joining it to their own labor in the earth and to their stubborn agrarian independence. But in the acceptance of indebtedness as an operating principle in society, Randolph thought, modernity has brought about a corruption in the very nature of people. In a speech opposing a new state constitution for Virginia in 1829, Randolph argued that "people are changed from what they have been." "I say that the character of the good old Virginia planter—the man who owned from five to twenty slaves, or less, who lived by hard work, and who paid his debts, is passed away. A new order of things is come. The period has arrived of living by one's wits—of living by contracting debts that one cannot pay—and above all, of living by office-hunting." [7]

This and similar statements put a mournful period to the errand into paradise, or a "paradise improved," that had been announced a century and a quarter earlier by Robert Beverley. A dark nostalgia grew steadily in Randolph's mind, and toward the end of his life he was thought to be insane. He died in a strange room in Philadelphia, exclaiming, "Remorse! Remorse!" As far as anybody has discerned, he cried out in despair over no particular sin either of omission or of commission. It was as though a sense of regret of the pastness of the past overwhelmed him; as though he lamented some unredeemable apostasy to a former day his own age had committed. John Randolph's career symbolizes the increasing isolation of the Southern consciousness in its endeavor somehow to strike a balance between the need to divorce slavery from the vision of pastoral permanence and the radical necessity of incorporating slavery into the pastoral vision.

I think we may represent a second stage of the displacement of pastoral in the Southern mind by a subtle struggle appearing in a novel usually considered to be the prototypical novel of the literary plantation, John Pendleton Kennedy's *Swallow Barn: Or Life in the Old Dominion.* First published in 1831, two years before Randolph's death, this story may seem on the surface to be—as it is so often considered to be—a highly effective rendition of the nostalgic mode of pastoral. The plantation of

Frank Meriwether is a transformation of the Southern
plantation into Arcadia; or, more nearly, it is the transformation of the plantation into the idealized order of
a pastoral squirearchy. Gentle and somewhat comical,
Frank Meriwether is an American cousin of the English
squire, lord over a less glamorous but a more kindly and
far more pleasant ancestral estate than ever existed in
England. Also, it is to be noted, the narrator of the story,
Mark Littleton, is a New Yorker who is visiting Swallow
Barn. Thus we have introduced an element more explic-
itly stressed in Old World pastoral than in nineteenth-
century American pastoral: the tension between city and
country. But examining *Swallow Barn* carefully, we note
that this tension remains so relaxed that it is scarcely
visible. The basic tension which holds the story together
is altogether different. This is a conflict between the
institution of slavery and the pastoral image of Swallow
Barn.

Kennedy's intention may appear to be to assimilate
slavery to an image of pastoral permanence by depicting
an "organic" relationship between master and slave.
The two will exist in harmony always; or, at any rate,
until that distant time when, as Meriwether thinks, it will
be possible for the slaves to become free agents. Such
a vision of harmony is apparently congenial to Littleton's
preconceived sentimental opinion of the plantation order, but nonetheless his reaction to the order of life
evidenced at Swallow Barn is ambivalent. For one thing,
as William R. Taylor has shrewdly observed in *Cavalier
and Yankee,* the narrator is aware of its phony feudalism,
and his account of his visit is marked in numerous places
by a satirical tone. Taylor has reference to various
characterizations by the narrator and to his delight in
such episodes as the one in which Bel Tracy, a young
lady much smitten with the days of chivalry, attempts the

art of falconry, "using an uncooperative hawk as her falcon and a bewildered Negro boy as her falconer." Mingling satire with sentimentality, Kennedy's narrator is, as Taylor observes, "an emotional Indian giver." He gives "a flattering image of 'feudal' Virginia," then withdraws "it smilingly." [9]

Kennedy plainly wants to suggest that slavery resists embodiment in the hierarchical pattern of society that is in the minds of the masters. More importantly, I think, Kennedy insinuates the suggestion, whether deliberately or not, that the slaves dominate the life of the plantation. In English pastoralism the strategy is to present the image of the manor without allowing the labor force, the peasantry, to appear in it, or if they do, to place them so far in the background that they have no faces. But in Kennedy's novel the slaves from the beginning have a high degree of visibility. Not only this, in one or two instances they serve to suggest the fallibility of the order the master class has established, or imagines it has established, by parodying its manners. Old Jupiter, the "King of the Quarter," is one of Meriwether's pets. He has his own horse, wears a *chapeau de bras,* and has demanded a pair of spurs. A parody of Meriwether, he possesses the moral authority of the clown. A more significant clown, however, appears at the beginning of *Swallow Barn;* and although his appearance is brief, he is a presence throughout the story. He is the outrider who conducts Littleton into the world of the plantation, a venerable free Negro named Scipio, who before the American Revolution was "a retainer in some of the feudal establishments of the low countries." "From some aristocratic conceit of elegance," Scipio wears "a ragged regimental coat, still jagged with some points of tarnished scarlet" —a coat which probably had been worn by an officer in the Revolution; and he makes a ridiculous figure as he bestrides "a short, thick-set pony, with an amazingly rough trot" and prods him with a rusty spur buckled onto one of his bare, bony feet. But what he says to Littleton is of the essence of wisdom.

He expatiated with a wonderful relish upon the splendors of the old-fashioned style in that part of the country; and told me very pathetically, how the estates were cut up, and what old people had died off, and how much he felt himself alone in the present times,—which particulars he interlarded with sundry sage remarks, imparting an affectionate attachment to the old school, of which he considered himself no unworthy survivor. He concluded these disquisitions with a reflection that amused me by its profundity—and which doubtless he had picked up from some popular orator: "When they change the circumstance, they alter the case." My expression of assent to this aphorism awoke all his vanity,—for after pondering a moment upon it, he shook his head archly as he added,—"People think old Scipio a fool, because he's got sense," and, thereupon, the old fellow laughed till the tears came into his eyes.[10]

Scipio is a parody of a standard figure of American nostalgia, the "old school" man—the relic who in far retrospect views an ordered world of the past—in this case a grand pastoral aristocracy which has been sadly altered by the American Revolution. To survive in the disorderly present, Scipio wears the trappings of the past like a clown. He has acquired a secret and superior wisdom: historical change is certain and irreversible and cannot be contained in any illusion of restored authority. At the same time in his comical parody of the past, Scipio implies that the "palmy days" he so reveres may never have been more than illusory. A pastoral clown—an anomalous figure, the free Negro, dispossessed of his

servitude and outside the garden of the chattel—Scipio
conducts Littleton, a different kind of outsider, into the
plantation garden, warning him that the case has been
altered, and in offering him the wisdom of the fool in-
timating that Littleton may discern the hidden or inner
meaning of the garden: that at its heart is a pathos of
order.

This pathos is revealed most strikingly in two episodes
near the conclusion of Kennedy's novel: one in which
Meriwether conducts Littleton on a tour of the slave
quarters and another, immediately following, in which
Meriwether takes his guest to visit an aged slave named
Lucy, whose "cottage was removed from the rest of the
cabins, and seemed to sleep in the shade of a wood upon
the skirts of which it was situated." [12]

When he sees the slaves in their quarters, Littleton is
impressed with their secure domestic situation. He is led
to reflect that they constitute a "parasitical" people in
a benevolently protected stage of transition from barba-
rism to civilization. They are, Littleton observes to his
host, the happiest laborers he has seen. Whereupon
Meriwether delivers a speech on the nature and necessity
of slavery as it exists in the South. Taking as his underlying thesis the idea of the Southern slavery system as a
transitional stage in the development of the African, the
master of Swallow Barn advances to the point of suggesting that this process could be enhanced by mitigating the
chattel status of the slave. Specifically he would like to
see the enactment of laws to "recognize and regulate"
marriages among slaves and to prevent the separation
of husband and wife by sale and even to forbid "the
coercive separation of children from the mother—at
least during the period when one requires the care of the
other." Another, and more daring, reform Meriwether
has in mind involves the idea of establishing "by law, an

upper or privileged class of slaves—selecting them from
the most deserving, above the age of forty-five years."
Meriwether would endue these "with something of feudal character." He explains that the privileged class
would be "entitled to hold small tracts of land under
their masters, rendering for it a certain rent, payable
either in personal service or money." Although
Meriwether does not say so, it is clear that as "tenants
in socage" the privileged class would be removed from
chattel servitude and elevated to something approaching
a peasantry.[11] What lies behind Meriwether's proposal
to make a "feudatory" of the slave is no doubt not simply
benevolence. In part it is inspired by the need felt by the
Southern literary mind, as exemplified in Kennedy, to
counter the antipastoral character of the Southern slavery system by giving the chattel a pastoral relation to
the land. Thus Meriwether has a vision of a pastoral,
quasi-slave community at the center of the garden of
the chattel.

Interestingly enough, when Littleton accepts Meriwether's invitation to walk beyond the limits of the slave
quarters for a visit to "old Lucy," he enters a garden
within the garden, a pleasant place situated along a little
creek and made more beautiful by a "gay luxuriance" of
flowers planted within the enclosure before Lucy's cottage. This little world apart, it turns out, represents the
relic of Meriwether's first feudatory act. Lucy is the
widow of Luke, who had been a faithful body servant of
Captain Hazard (Littleton's uncle and master of Swallow
Barn before Meriwether) during Hazard's service in the
American Revolution. After the war, Luke, enjoying
"familiar but respectful intimacy with his master," had
become his consultant on "many lesser matters relating
to the estate." Hazard had thought about giving him his
freedom but valuing Luke too greatly to give him "an

unavailing, formal grant of manumission," had given "him a few acres of ground in the neighbourhood of the Quarter, and provided him with a comfortable cabin." The youngest child of the union of Lucy and Luke was a boy named Abe, a child singular in appearance; for instead of the African physiognomy of his brothers and sisters, he bears the features "of the negroes of the West Indies," which means that he has the facial features associated with the white race. Abe is also unlike his brothers and sisters in that he turns out to be a bad actor, taking up with a "band of out-lying negroes, who had secured themselves for some weeks, in the fastnesses of the low-country swamps, from whence they annoyed the vicinity by nocturnal incursions of the most lawless character." Although these were apparently more in the nature of pilfering expeditions than acts of rebellion, Meriwether has of course to remove Abe from the plantation community. He decides to do this in an enlightened way. To take advantage of Abe's "active, intelligent and intrepid character," he binds him over to the service of a Chesapeake pilot. On board the pilot sloop *Flying-Fish* Abe applies himself to the arts of sailing with enthusiasm and soon becomes an unusually fine sailor, the repression he had felt on land released in the joy of riding the free winds of the sea. On the night of a great storm he volunteers to attempt to save the crew and passengers of a ship which is going to pieces on a reef. With an all-black crew, also volunteers, Abe, against the advice of veteran seamen, puts out into the storm. The *Flying-Fish* is lost with all hands, save for one sailor who tells the tale.[13]

Why Kennedy brings in the story of Luke and Lucy and Abe is not altogether apparent, as indeed very little in *Swallow Barn* is plainly apparent. The episode belongs to the pattern of ambivalence that comprises the inner structure of a work that puzzled its author himself. Looking back on it after twenty years, he decided he had written a desultory work: "Our old friend Polonious had nearly hit it in his rigmarole of 'pastoral-comical, tragical-comical-historical-pastoral'—which, saving 'the tragical,' may well make up my schedule." [14] But Kennedy probably attempted to put in a little of the "tragical" too in the Lucy episode. Although it is called "A Negro Mother," this episode finds its chief focus in Abe; and instead of attempting merely, as Littleton says, to show that "the picturesque" is present in "the development of [the] habit and feelings" of a people of "unpretending lowliness," it deals covertly with the rebellion of a slave's spirit. Littleton exclaims about "the gallant sight" of "such heroism shining out in a humble slave of the Old Dominion." [15] But what Abe has done he has done out of a fierce pride in his own courage and daring. He wants to prove that he is braver than the white sailors. And not only this. Abe's voluntary acceptance of the rescue mission is a suicidal act; he is too skilled in sailing not to understand that venturing forth is "certain doom." The mission gains nothing but the death of himself and his crew of blacks, which would appear to be what they wanted.

The treatment of Abe in *Swallow Barn* comes close to suggesting that out of the heart of the garden of the chattel in its most idealized image there might come forth a slave who, potentially at any rate, could become an apostatic figure—a slave possessed of the conviction that slavery is an apostasy to freedom and who yearns, possibly without articulate consciousness, to transform the garden of the chattel into a dominion of pastoral freedom, an Eden of freed slaves. But at the same time the treatment of Abe suggests that when this latent figure of alienation from the dominion of the masters appears in the imagination of the writer, the writer must suppress him. In his account of Abe, Littleton interprets him as an example of the slave who is in a perfect relationship with his masters. He gives his life in their service.

In sum, it would seem, *Swallow Barn* is an uncertain attempt at a pastoral ratification of slavery. In the attempt the novel discloses a pathos of pastoral order which occurs in the effort of the Southern literary imagination to institutionalize chattel slavery in the name of pastoral.

The third stage in the antebellum Southern experience of alienation through the frustration of the pastoral consciousness is represented by a struggle both fully to apprehend and fully to accept the meaning of the garden of the chattel: that as a unique reaction against modernity slavery has dispossessed the garden of the Western pastoral imagination. This stage occupies the span of years from the early 1830s until the end of the War for Southern Independence. During this period the "positive good" argument for slavery predominated, holding that if slavery is to be supported it cannot be upheld as a negative good. It must take over the mind of the supporter in a total way; slavery must be identified with the independence of the master's mind. Independence of mind is dependent on slavery, not simply because it is necessary to leisure but because maintenance of slavery is necessary to the maintenance of the very will to freedom on the part of the masters. The Southern reaction to modernity must assume a novel truth: modernity is an apostasy to slavery.

Whether or not the bulk of the Southern proslavery argument written in the mid-nineteenth century fully supports an affirmation of slavery is doubtful. In a bril-

liant contrary analysis, David Donald has argued that this
large body of writing is dominated by nostalgia for a
world that never was.[16] As I have made evident, I incline
to the view—not necessarily antithetical to Donald's—
that as a body of work by a Southern clerisy it represents
a literature of radical alienation from modernity. Although far different from the New England writings, in
this respect it is analogous in its historical role to the
literature produced by, in Emerson's term, New England's "soldiery of dissent." An expression of a culture
of alienation in the South, it is not, primarily at any rate,
an endeavor to oppose the disintegrating forces of modern history with a dream of a restoration of "the good
old days." It is an attempt to envision a uniquely reactionary philosophy of society. Such an attempt called for
leaders of thought who would serve not simply as its
leading voices but as distillers of its spirit—who altogether in their personal lives, as well as in their speeches
and writings, would embody the movement in charis-
matic essence. Leaders comparable in power to such
New England figures as William Ellery Channing, Emerson, Theodore Parker, and others who were descended
from the old ministry of the New England garden. Of a
number of roughly comparable figures who appeared in
the South, I think we may in the abbreviated schema I
am developing focus on the career of only one, William
Gilmore Simms. Looked at with respect to (and respect
for) its underlying meaning, the career of Simms takes
on the quality of a story of the nineteenth-century man
of letters foiled in a quest to become a heroic and redemptive literary figure.

Simms had, he said of himself, "a mind whose strong-
est passion is that of letters."[17] With furious energy he
wrote over eighty books, involved himself endlessly in
literary enterprises of one kind or another, carried on a

large correspondence, collected a splendid library, and, to be sure, endeavored more earnestly than any other man of letters of his time to establish a profession of letters in the South. As nearly as the South had a center in the Republic of Letters following the age when Monticello was such a place, Simms's plantation (called Woodlands) was it. It is hardly too much to say that in a literary sense the Age of Jefferson was succeeded by the Age of William Gilmore Simms. In a career larger and more complicated than we have acknowledged in literary history, Simms expressed the tone and quality of an intellectual and literary epoch. In contrast to Jefferson, Simms experienced the inner imperative of the literary existence as it came to be known in the nineteenth century: the need to authenticate the literary existence through the intimacy of the writer's personal suffering in a world hostile, or worse, indifferent to what he represents. No Southern writer (save Poe) had a more vivid education than Simms in the struggle of the writer to make a valid personal representation in his society of the independence and autonomy of the literary intellect. For example, we find Simms saying in 1845, and at a time when his reputation as a writer had become well established and he might well have had a satisfaction in his labors: "I have worked in the face of fortune and many foes. I have never known what was cordial sympathy, in any of my pursuits among men. I have been an exile from my birth, and have learned nothing but to drudge with little hope, and to think and feel and act for myself. Through painful necessities I have come to the acquisition of an Independent Mind." [18] A couple of years later, Simms is thinking about leaving the South for good. "Here I am nothing & can be & do nothing. The South don't care a d—n for literature or art. Your best neighbour & kindred never think to buy books. They will bor-

row from you & beg, but the same man who will always
have his wine, has no idea of a library. You will write for
& defend their institutions in vain. They will not pay the
expense of printing your essays." [19] Some ten years later
Simms is writing about being compelled to sell some rare
volumes in his extensive library to meet the necessities
of existence: "Milton for a bushel of corn, Shakespeare
for a bunch of onions, Chaucer for a string of fish, and
Bacon for a barrell of beans, &c!!" [20]

When we place such self-conscious recognitions of his
role as writer in the context of Simms's total aspirations
and activities, we find that his consciousness of himself
as a man of letters is entangled with his identification of
himself as the representative of an entire social order
existing in alienation from modern history. What makes
Poe's case as a Southern writer special as compared to
Simms's—or what makes Simms's case special as compared to Poe's if you will—is that in Simms's the modern
effort to ratify the life of the writer in the face of real or
fancied opposition by society was integrally connected
to an effort to authenticate the historical existence of the
South as a special historical case—a chosen nation.
Simms began to make this connection early in his career
in an idealization of Southern society which is an answer
to Harriet Martineau's aspersions on slavery in the South
in her *Society in America* (1837). Employing a conception
of society as a hierarchy of proper degree, Simms argued
in an essay in the *Southern Literary Messenger* in 1837 that
the founders of the Republic interpreted democracy not
as social leveling but as "the harmony of the moral
world." Liberty is defined by the moral and intellectual
capacities, by the powers of mind. *"He is a freeman, whatever his condition, who fills his proper place. He is a slave only,
who is forced into a position in society below the claims of his
intellect. He cannot but be a tyrant who is found in a position*

*for which his mind is unprepared, and to which it is inferior."*
Holding that the Negro is completely unprepared for
freedom, Simms declares that the slaveholders of the
South have a holy contract with God to be the stewards
of their African slaves. Having "the moral and animal
guardianship of an ignorant and irresponsible people
under their control," they "are the great moral conserva-
tors, in one powerful interest, of the entire world."
Simms declares: "There is no propriety in the application of the name of the slave to the servile of the south.
He is under no despotic power. There are laws which
protect him, *in his place,* as inflexible as those which his
proprietorship is required to obey, *in his place. Providence
has placed him in our hands, for his good, and has paid us from
his labor for our guardianship."*[21] Although there is nothing
original in Simms's argument that slavery devolves upon
the masters as "a sacred duty, undertaken to God and
man alike," it is a more comprehensive motive in
Simms's imagination of the role of the Southern writer
than it is in the conceptualization of the role in the mind
of any of his contemporaries. Simms attempted in his
career as a critic and storyteller to become a prophet and
priest of a Southern literary covenant—to realize the
garden of the chattel in a vision, if not in actuality, as
a covenanted garden. He endeavored, especially as a
novelist, to symbolize the culture of alienation in the
pastoral metaphor of a Southern garden of permanence opposed to the modern dispensation of endless
alteration.

I make these assertions with a stout simplicity, when
I know they cannot be proved through simple explica-
tion. But falling back on the reserved intention of the
present remarks, let me refer, and this briefly, to one
novel by Simms. This is *Woodcraft,* which along with *Swallow Barn* is probably the most significant fiction written

in the antebellum South. Fifth in the series of seven
novels Simms wrote about South Carolina in the Revolution, it is the final one with respect to the chronology of
events depicted in the stories. In this part of the Revolutionary saga, Porgy, a corpulent connoisseur of hominy
and hoe cakes but nonetheless a highly sensitive, philosophical, and indeed poetic planter, and Tom, his faithful body servant and cook, return to a plantation world
devastated by war. After a series of adventures and
misadventures, they at length become reestablished on
Porgy's plantation, Glen-Eberley, and at the end of the
story have in prospect lives of peace and plenty. But the
prospect is a strangely constricted one, and the way in
which Simms arrives at it requires comment.

One of Simms's key concerns in *Woodcraft*, a novel
written with his usual rapidity, is to provide an answer
to Harriet Beecher Stowe's notorious *Uncle Tom's Cabin*,
a novel published earlier the same year (1852). The heart
of the answer is the further development of the relationship between Porgy and Tom, a master-slave connection
explored in Simms's previous stories of the Revolutionary epoch. In *Woodcraft* the relationship of Tom and
Porgy is obviously intended to be placed opposite that
Mrs. Stowe explores in the case of Uncle Tom and his
masters.

One thing that is so interesting about *Uncle Tom's Cabin*
is the way in which as the story moves toward its climax
Mrs. Stowe transforms the garden of the chattel into a
horrifying symbol of modernity, the plantation of Simon
Legree. Formerly the home of a Southern "gentleman
of opulence and taste," who has died insolvent, it has
been acquired by Legree, the cruel overseer of Yankee
extraction, to use "as he did everything else, merely as
an implement for money-making"; and it has become a
place of pastoral desolation: the lawn, shrubs, and flow-

ers are forsaken, "a large garden was now grown over
with weeds," "the ground littered with broken pails,
cobs of corn, and other slovenly remains." In the dark
and ruined mansion in which Legree dwells the wallpa-
per is "defaced in spots, by slops of beer and wine; or
garnished with chalk memorandums, and long sums
footed up, as if somebody had been practising arithmetic
there." [22] This wasteland world, Mrs. Stowe implies, is
but a Southern version of the ruthless marketplace society which dominates the nation. Living in the inner
estrangement from this world, is the kindly, neurotic,
agnostic, and poetic planter, Augustine St. Clare.
Stabbed with a bowie knife while trying to separate two
intoxicated gentlemen in a cafe brawl, the dying St. Clare
refuses a clergyman but entreats Tom to pray for him.
In doing so Tom becomes the priest of St. Clare's salvation from the wasteland. Filled anew with the piety of his
childhood, the Louisiana planter goes through "the
gates of eternity" exclaiming "Mother!" [23] Tom—who
later on dies a martyr to freedom in the spiritual wasteland ruled by the precarpetbagging, pre-Snopes Legree,
having forgiven Sambo and Quimbo (the degraded black
minions of Legree) for torturing him—saves St. Clare
from the extreme isolation of mind and spirit which has
blocked his participation in life. This is an isolation
caused by the suppression of his hatred of his own society; for even though he despises slavery, St. Clare must
accept it. The Southern version of the culture of alienation, which is intimated in the sensibility of St. Clare,
cannot redeem him. Harriet Beecher Stowe suggests that
the Southerner lives in a state of dependence of mind—
that the "peculiar institution" prohibits any independence of mind or redemptive reaction to modernity. She
not only suggests that the slave South cannot redeem
modernity but that the gardener in the Southern garden,

as represented by Sambo and Quimbo, can be claimed by modernity. The Southern pastoral covenant is in truth an illusion, or worse, a falsification.

In the salvation of St. Clare by Uncle Tom—who, it must be remembered, earnestly desires his freedom from St. Clare in spite of his affection for his master—the chattel becomes an instrument of the New England literary covenant, of, that is, the nineteenth-century literary fulfillment of the redemptive mission of the Puritans. Harriet Beecher Stowe brings the slave South into the scope of this mission more successfully than any other New England writer. In a sense St. Clare and Legree are opposing sides of the New England world as well as of the Southern, for St. Clare's father had employed "a great, tall, slab-sided, two-fisted renegade son of Vermont" as the hard, brutal overseer of the five hundred Negroes on his Louisiana plantation. [24] Moreover, St. Clare had spent much of his boyhood in Vermont on a prosperous farm owned by his uncle, his father's brother. (The St. Clare brothers were from Canada, one having settled in Vermont, the other in Louisiana.) Did not Mrs. Stowe's strength derive fundamentally from her role as an apostatic figure in the New England garden? From her mission to redeem a New England that accepted chattel slavery as a fact of the economic and political operation of the United States? When Tom liberates the consciousness of St. Clare, a figure resembling the romantic artist, from a bondage to a society dominated by money and power, he is incorporated into the expression of the New England culture of alienation and becomes one of its heroes.

It is difficult to estimate the extent to which Simms took in the meaning of *Uncle Tom's Cabin,* but the development of the Porgy-Tom relationship in *Woodcraft* is a significant response to Mrs. Stowe's portrayal of the Uncle Tom–St. Clare–Legree relationship.

Sorely in debt, Porgy stands the chance of losing Tom to his debtors. Early in the course of the story Porgy declares to Lance, one of his military aides, that he will kill Tom rather than let him pass into the hands of an unworthy master: "I'll shoot *him*—him, Tom—in order to save him. The poor fellow has faithfully served a gentleman. He shall never fall into the hands of a scamp. I'll sacrifice him as a burnt-offering for my sins and his own. Tom, I'm thinking would rather die my slave, than live a thousand years under another owner." [25] Later Porgy declares the same intention directly to Tom, but in this instance he urges upon a horrified Tom an act of self-destruction if circumstances should prevent Porgy from killing him. At the end of the story Tom, offered his freedom by Porgy (who of course knows that Tom will reject "a gift of himself") makes plain the basis of his relationship with his master, Porgy, and Porgy's relation to him: "Ef I doesn't b'long to *you, you* b'long to *me!* . . . *You* b'long to *me* Tom, jes' as much as me Tom b'long to *you;* and you nebber guine git *you* free paper from me long as you lib." [26] Although all three of the scenes involving the expression of the absoluteness of the connection between Porgy and Tom are comical—turning in each case upon Porgy's need for Tom's culinary skill and Tom's pride in meeting the need—Tom's service at Porgy's table approaches a symbolization of a eucharistic union of the consciousness of the master and the slave. But it is Tom who offers the gifts; Tom who says that he dwells in his master and his master in him. If Porgy should do so, it would jeopardize the existence of the South. The Porgy-Tom relationship amounts to a reversal of the terms of the covenant: Tom—"the cook and proprietor of his master"—has acquired property in the consciousness of Porgy. Porgy is subject to his will. In some strange way Tom the chattel has become the priest of the garden. Through the mutual love of master and slave the garden of the chattel has been transcended; the purity of the errand into paradise has been restored, and at the end of the story the errand has been fulfilled. But it is a confusing and sterile fulfillment. Glen-Eberley presents to the world, it is true, the image of both "a well-managed household, in which the parties were all at peace with themselves and one another" and "a sort of center for the parish civilization," which draws "the gentry all round, within the sphere of its genial, yet provocative influences." At the ostensible center of this plantation pastoral is the figure of a genial, philosophical, poetic master, the redeemed Porgy, who, according to the author, rules his domain with a beneficent but "strong will." And yet it is clear that in reality Glen-Eberley is as much controlled by an illiterate slave as by the master, whose loss of freedom for love of his master is the redemption of a world. Glen-Eberley, moreover, is a world which has no future, for it has no female dimension. Tom says that he could never "be happy in house whar woman is de maussa," and Porgy, whose attitude toward marriage is always basically negative, finally gives up all attempts to get a wife, renouncing "the temptations of the flesh" he tells his male companions—Dr. Oakenburg, Sergeant Millhouse, and Tom—so that he can keep inviolate his relationship with them.[27] So Glen-Eberley, in contrast to the usual literary plantation, is not and is not ever to become a matriarchal community, the nursery of future generations. It is an all-male community, white and black—a world without issue doomed to come to an end with its present generation, that of the American Revolution.

What all this signifies I am not sure—an all-male plantation in the midst of a society which had not only fought to create a new nation for the sake of its posterity but which worshiped the family and faithfully practiced fecundity. Under the mask of the "comical-pastoral" Simms in *Woodcraft* hints, I think, at a deep vexation in the Southern writer's attempt to authenticate the South's historical existence as a slave society. Simms suggests that at the margins of his imagination there was an awareness of an ultimate irreconcilability of the Southern slavery system to the pastoral mode. He sensed that the logical end of striving to transform the scheme of chattel slavery into terms of the pastoral reaction to modern history would be to discover this; and that such a discovery would mean the ultimate dispossession of the pastoral mode in the Southern literary imagination.

It would reveal that the African chattel had come into the Southern garden of paradise as an intruder, dispossessing the garden of the Western pastoral imagination, transforming it into a garden of the chattel, and threatening to transform the South into an image of a completely nonpastoral character. It would reveal too the logic underlying the threat. The Southern political economy demanded that the dominion of chattel slavery be extended not only to areas beyond the borders of the original South but that it be extended within the social structure of the South itself. In other words, as George Fitzhugh, the most brilliant and ruthlessly logical mind of the Southern clerisy, argued, slavery to be fully recognized as the truth of a "slaveholders' world" must be extended nonracially to embrace the lower-class whites. The South must become a complete, self-contained slave society living in isolation from all free society and from the world marketplace—a nation apart.

Such a vision, Eugene D. Genovese argues persuasively in his *The World the Slaveholders Made,* was the full implication of the world view the Southerners struggled to achieve.[28] In this view the South would be independent of a world market and would fulfill its complete historical implication: a society totally reactionary against modern history, a precapitalist and prebourgeois society. Such a society, I have suggested, would not have been prior to any other society; it would have been more nearly a totally novel one. It would have required new modes of thinking and feeling and new modes of literary expression. A new kind of literary mind.

It is significant that as the pressures to complete the institutionalization of slavery grew in the South, Simms made some attempts to idealize slavery outside the context of the pastoral mode.

The Southern States [he wrote in 1860, for example] are all welded together by the institution of African slavery —an institution which has done more for philanthropy and humanity in one year than ever has been achieved by all the professional philanthropists of Europe and America in one hundred years: and this labor, in our genial climate, can be applied to all the industrial arts—to the construction of railroads—to the working of mills—in brief, to all the provinces of toil. Our water power never freezes, and it is abundant, our labor never times itself to short or long hours, and never *strikes,* impatient to share largely in the profits of the capitalists.[29]

Simms had glimpses at least of a South stripped of the pastoral ideal—of, we might say, the burden of the pastoral ideal—emerging in modern history as an isolated and total political economy. If he never admitted the necessity of incorporating the poor-white class in the South into the slavery system, Simms did see the need to make a more complete use of slavery in the Southern labor system. This demanded that the image of the South be transformed from that of a pastoral garden into that of an integrated and autonomous agricultural-industrial world. But, however precariously, Simms remained faithful to the pastoral motive and thus to the institutional sense of letters and literature. One reason why a new mind could not come into being in the South was that the literary mind—as exemplified by a Simms —could not effectively imagine itself as a novel mind. It could not imagine the need to do so. And there is nothing strange in this; for literature has been, and may even yet be, a continuum. Literary novelty can only be relative to the continuity of literature, and what may seem to be radical literary innovations, such as James Joyce's *Finnegans Wake,* turn out to be basically inherent in the continuity. George Fitzhugh was singular in the remorseless logic with which he pursued the uniqueness of the Southern relation to history; dismissing the pastoral pieties as nonsense, he was alone in so doing. At the expense of seeing slavery realistically as an institution outside the domain of Western pastoral, the Southern literati held onto the literary mind.

In one of the final scenes in *Woodcraft,* Porgy, the garrulous camp philosopher and storyteller, sits in the midst of his illusory, masculine world of pastoral permanence regaling the gentry with narratives "of the experiences through which he had gone, delivering history and biography and opinion." [30] It is a scene symbolizing the pastoral plantation as the homeland of the literary mind, and thus represents a fulfillment of the redemptive literary reaction to modernity by a Southern version of the culture of alienation. But the expense of the scene as we calculate it in terms of the emotional economy of Simms's novel is the subversion of the Southern system of chattel slavery. The relationship of Porgy and Tom in *Woodcraft* represents a pathos of pastoral order created by the struggle of the antebellum Southern literary mind to make the advocacy of slavery a mode of alienation; that is, to join the defense of slavery to the effort to

THREE

# The Southern Recovery of Memory and History

"There is no such thing really as was, because the past is."
—William Faulkner

IN THE CONCLUDING DISCUSSION I SHALL MAKE SOME OB-
servations on the subject of the culture of alienation as
this has manifested itself in the twentieth-century South.
By the term *culture of alienation,* as I have indicated, I
mean modern literature; or, more inclusively, the modern literary mind—that segment of the general culture
which for nearly two centuries has been characterized by
its opposition to modernity. I refer particularly to its
large expression of discontent with the emphasis modern societies place on machines and consumption as a
debasement of the humanity of man; to its registration
of the loss of the classical-Christian values of the Western world; and its endeavor, marked by an ironic consciousness of the futility of the effort, to arrest the de-
humanization considered to be inherent in the
industrial-technological process.

In its more superficial aspect the Southern version of the
culture of alienation in the twentieth century has appeared to advocate a restoration of the pastoral mode
of existence represented by an idealized Old South. The

noted Agrarian movement of the late 1920s has been seen as a kind of literal attempt to oppose the loss of a green and pleasant agricultural nation, divested more or less of the component of slavery, to the triumph of a grey and harsh industrial nation in the North. Or Faulkner, who stood apart from all movements, has been viewed as a lonely agrarian protesting American industrialism and lamenting a lost pastoral South. But such views are narrowly conceived. In the twentieth century the Southern sense of literary alienation has been fully joined to the wider literary and artistic opposition to modernity.

Long before this happened the Southern literary mind had been released by the failure of the Southern War for Independence from the special character of its reaction to modernity in the first half of the nineteenth century— that is, from its unique struggle to associate the culture of alienation with its covenant with slavery. But this un-shackling of the mind did not represent a complete loss of the antebellum experience of alienation. As the liter-ary imagination of the South entered into a search for a renewed image of its meaning amid the disorders inaugurating the present century—including the Span-ish-American War and the First World War—it discov-ered a congruence of the Old South experience of alien-ation and the general character of the culture of alienation being formed in Western civilization by the humanistic reaction to modernity.

If any Southern writer in antebellum times clearly an-ticipated this discovery, it was Edgar Allan Poe—as I have emphasized a special case of the Southern writer, the only one who came intimately into the knowledge of a developing alienation in the Western literary mind. The record of Poe's anticipation appears throughout his writings, the most appropriate, and graphic, instance in the context of the present remarks being perhaps "The Fall of the House of Usher." First published in 1839, this famous story has been subjected to myriad interpretations, among these being the conception of the story as a symbolization of the self-destruction of the Southern aristocracy. In spite of the fact that Roderick Usher is not a slave master (the narrator refers to Usher's servants as "the peasantry"), this is a plausible and probable meaning. If the image of Usher's somber and dreary garden, dominated by a melancholy mansion beside a "black and lurid tarn," is a Gothic inversion of the harmony of the standard English pastoral domain, it can as easily be an inversion of John Pendleton Kennedy's Swallow Barn. The Southern imagination identified the plantation with the English manor. But in this identification, as I have remarked elsewhere, the Southern literary mind sought not simply a satisfying image of the Southern social order but an image of its own existence—an image of the plantation as the homeland of the literary mind. In a fundamental sense "The Fall of the House of Usher" may be taken, I think, as a fantasy of the plantation homeland of the antebellum literary mind. Regarded in this way the story discovers this mind as a symbol of the culture of alienation.

Poe obviously conceived Usher in some wise as a portrait of the literary artist. Painter and musician, he is primarily a poet. He is as well a historian of sorts, an inquirer principally into the history of the supernatural and the occult. But in all his artistic composition and reading he is involved purely with himself; he is obsessed with an agonizing consciousness of his own consciousness. This in essence is the nature of the "anomalous species of terror" to which his friend, the narrator, finds Usher "a bounden slave." "I shall perish," Usher exclaims.

I must *perish* in this deplorable folly. Thus, thus, and not
otherwise, shall I be lost. I dread the events of the future,
not in themselves, but in their results. I shudder at the
thought of any, even the most trivial incident, which may
operate upon this intolerable agitation of soul. I have,
indeed, no abhorrence of danger, except in its absolute
effect,—in terror. In this unnerved, in this pitiable condition, I feel that the period will sooner or later arrive when
I must abandon life and reason together in some struggle
with the grim phantasm, FEAR.

Usher's hypersensitivity to the future, his apprehension
about how events yet to happen may affect his mind, is
paralleled by his sense of an undefined yet absolutely
frightening continuity his mind has with the past: by, as
the narrator puts it, "that silent yet importunate and
terrible influence which for centuries had moulded the
destinies of his family, and which made *him* what I now
saw him,—what he was." This influence, which Usher
believes in with "an earnest abandon of . . . persua-
sion," exudes, he thinks, from the sentience of the "gray
stones of the home of his forefathers." [1] Usher's imagination of the past and the future has come to center
entirely in his own existence; he lacks the capacity to
apprehend his possible relation to a community of other
human beings. Although he recognizes his own terrible
folly, he has made and sealed a covenant with the self
as the sole source of memory and the total meaning of
history. Seeing Usher "enchained" or, more exactly, en-
tombed in the house secluded in the depths of an un-
specified landscape, we realize that his mind is in fact the
scene of the story.

It is not too much to say that in Usher's fearful intro-
version the symbolic identification between the Southern dream of an enclosed plantation world—the "garden
of the chattel" I have ironically called it—and the literary

mind has become in an awesome manner complete.
Standing apart from the world view of the South in which
he had been reared and yet still a part of it (an advocate
of the slavery system), Poe—a literary genius who like
Petrarch and Rousseau was a "world historical neurotic" [2]—perceived, whether consciously or not, the fundamental meaning of the image of the homeland of the
Old South literary mind as a garden of pastoral permanence. It was a metaphor of a general condition of the
literary mind which was becoming evident by the mid-
nineteenth century. As the opposition of the culture of
alienation to modernity assumed more definitive propor-
tions, the literary consciousness was undergoing an
alienation from itself—that is, from its own history and
traditions—from the value system of memory and history
represented by the Christian and humanistic cultural
community. "The Fall of the House of Usher," whatever
else it means, can be taken as a symbol of this estrangement of the literary mind from itself. Usher's traumatic
relation to the past represents not simply a lapse from,
but a solipsistic corruption of, the continuity and authority of the past in the literary consciousness.

Although some of them had little enough use for Poe,
Southern writers of the 1920s and 1930s essentially discovered what Poe had discovered around seventy-five
years before: that in its experience of alienation as a
pastoral reaction to modernity, in its devotion to the
plantation image, the Southern literary mind had engaged in a withdrawal from memory and history. In
stronger terms, it had committed an apostasy to memory
and history. Like Poe, the Southern writers of the post–
First World War age—writers as well educated in literature as Poe—became aware that a kind of degradation
of memory and history was occurring in the general opposition of the literary mind to modernity, resulting in

a tendency of the literary consciousness to become isolated from its corporate relation to the cultural past. Southern writers beginning with, for example, Allen Tate and William Faulkner—and in this unlike the dark diagnostician of cultural illness, Poe—inaugurated a struggle to comprehend the nature of memory and history, and to assert the redemptive meaning of the classical-Christian past in its bearing on the present. The Southern literary mind which had once sought to symbolize its opposition to modernity in an image of pastoral permanence now began to seek to symbolize this antagonism in an image of a recovery—a restoration, perhaps a reconstruction—of memory and history. The expression of this quest has been in considerable measure responsible for what we have come to call the Southern Literary Renaissance—a flowering of literature in fiction and criticism, and to a somewhat lesser extent in poetry, that rivals the nineteenth-century New England efflorescence. It has been a complex expression. But I think we can see from the perspective of the 1970s that it has occurred in two major stages. The first was more or less contained within the years from the early 1920s to about 1950, the period of the end of the Second World War and the beginning of the Cold War (to be followed by all these years of small, deadly hot wars, the most ruinous conflicts morally and spiritually since the religious wars of the sixteenth and seventeenth centuries). This period is one in which Southern writing records an attempted reconstruction of the meaning of the past by the literary mind: a struggle to arrest the disintegration of memory and history by sophisticated writers who recognize their motive as one which is part and parcel of a larger endeavor to reconstruct the Western literary tradition. The second stage, the end of which has probably not yet been reached, is a period in which Southern writing tends to record the breakdown of the endeavor in reconstruction and to suggest, moreover, that the process of the destruction of memory and history within the literary mind symbolized by Poe in "The Fall of the House of Usher" cannot be halted; that inauguration of any attempt to establish a new literary covenant with the past is futile and that the only meaningful covenant for the latter-day writer is one with the self on terms generally defined as existential.

Let me approach the preoccupation with memory and history in the literature of the Southern Renaissance by characterizing it, somewhat loosely speaking, as a religious quest. I shall, playfully yet seriously, seize upon a central text of this movement, together with two commentaries on the text. The text is taken from chapter 9 of Faulkner's *Intruder in the Dust* (1948). Its context is a passage in which Chick Mallison, arriving at the crucial moment when he must decide what to do about the threatened lynching of the Negro Lucas Beauchamp, discovers a reference for his crisis of soul in the remembrance of what he had heard his uncle, the lawyer Gavin Stevens, say to him about the meaning of the Battle of Gettysburg in the Southern consciousness.

> It's all *now* you see. Yesterday wont be over until tomorrow and tomorrow began ten thousand years ago. For every Southern boy fourteen years old, not once but whenever he wants it, there is the instant when it's still not yet two o'clock on that July afternoon in 1863, the brigades are in position behind the rail fence, the guns are laid and ready in the woods, and the furled flags are already loosened to break out, and Pickett himself with his long oiled ringlets and his hat in one hand probably and his sword in the other looking up the hill waiting for Longstreet to give the word and it's all in the balance,

it hasn't happened yet, it hasn't even begun yet, it not
only hasn't begun yet but there is still time for it not to
begin against that position and those circumstances
which made more men than Garnett and Kemper and
Armstead [*sic*] and Wilcox look grave yet it's going to
begin, we all know that, we have come too far with too
much at stake and that moment doesn't need even a
fourteen-year-old boy to think *This time. Maybe this time*
with all this much to lose and all this much to gain:
Pennsylvania, Maryland, the world, the golden dome of
Washington itself to crown with desperate and unbeliev-
able victory the gamble, the cast made two years ago; or
to anyone who ever sailed even a skiff under a quilt sail,
the moment in 1492 when somebody thought *This is it:*
the absolute edge of no return, to turn back now and
make home or sail irrevocably on and either find land or
plunge over the world's roaring rim.[3]

I should like to move from my text to the first commentary on *Intruder in the Dust*. It is from a brilliant essay
by Andrew Lytle on Faulkner's novel. In the course of
his remarks Lytle says:

There is for any Southern writer of imagination an ines-
capable preoccupation with his native scene and especially with its historic predicament. He can no more escape it than a Renaissance painter could escape painting
Her Ladyship the Virgin and the Court of Angels. He has
been made to feel too sharply his uniqueness and the
uniqueness of his society in the modern world. His self-
consciousness does for him what blindness did for
Homer. He has been forced to achieve aesthetic distance.
It is this which gives to the boy protagonist in the book
the authority for his undertaking (a cult hero almost) and
allows him to absorb into the working out of his fate the
entire set of complex relationships which represent the
contradictions, the mixed virtues and vices, the agonies
even of the Southern sensibility, containing a vision at
once objective and involved: the poet-prophet who de-

fines a civilization bereft of historic destiny but which refuses the role.[4]

Just before saying this Lytle has been dealing with the essential plot of *Intruder in the Dust:* the dilemma Chick Mallison is in because he feels that Lucas Beauchamp by subtly denying him (a white boy) his racial preeminence has denied him his manhood, and thus, if ever so slightly, violated the order of their world; although at the same time Chick knows that the lynching of Lucas will be a violation of this community more destructive than his personal resentment of Lucas. Lytle further observes: "In one sense the historic isolation of the Southern culture by a victorious and hostile force serves for the fateful drive of the story: is at once the cause for action and the clue to its meaning. By focusing it in the moral destiny of a boy, the story becomes dramatic instead of didactic: that is, a novel and not propaganda." [5]

I shall now turn to a second commentary on my text. An indirect one, it is from a comment on Southern fiction in one of Allen Tate's central essays, "A Southern Mode of the Imagination." In this essay Tate describes a critical and highly fruitful shift in the Southern way of representing existence in words. The older Southern way was dominated by the rhetorical mode: "the mode of the speaker reporting in person an argument or an action in which he is not dramatically involved." This is the mode of the political imagination, and the political mind, Tate says, dominated the Southern mind (including the literary mind) for a long time. But in the period immediately following the First World War, he observes, the literary mind in the South changed its base of operations from rhetoric to dialectic.

The short answer to our question: How did this change come about? is that the South not only reentered the world with the first World War; it looked round and saw

for the first time since about 1830 that Yankees were not
to blame for everything. It looks like a simple discovery,
and it was; that is why it was difficult to make. The Southern legend, as Malcolm Cowley has called it, of defeat
and heroic frustration was taken over by a dozen or more
first-rate writers and converted into a universal myth of
the human condition. W. B. Yeats's great epigram points
to the nature of the shift from melodramatic rhetoric to
the dialectic of tragedy: "Out of the quarrel with others
we make rhetoric; out of the quarrel with ourselves, poetry." [6]

I appeal to the passages I have just quoted—to the
excerpt from *Intruder in the Dust* and to the comments by
Lytle and Tate—with a certain reverence. Indeed I think
they have a kind of authority that commands this, for
they are drawn from a body of story and critical commentary that collectively fulfills an act of revelation. Through
the art of the storyteller and of the critic, this corpus of
writing reveals a search for images of existence which
will express the truth that man's essential nature lies in
his possession of the moral community of memory and
history.

To return for a moment to my text in Faulkner. Gavin
Stevens in no way gives young Mallison a rational analysis of the boy's relation to the past. He does not say that
in his memory is a past that is approximately like the
present, that history somehow simply repeats itself. He
says that the crisis of the present is the crisis of the past
and the crisis of the past is the crisis of the present. The
relationship is not merely comparative or analogical but
integral. In that moment of time at Gettysburg when
General Robert E. Lee made an irrevocable commitment
to action, he was acting out of an inextricable web of
individual lives, private and public, and individual deci-
sions, private and public—out of, so to speak, the Bur-

kean community of the living, the dead, and the unborn. Gavin Stevens makes a poetic celebration of Chick's connection with the collectivity of memory and history that is often referred to unqualifiedly as "the past" but which involves time present and time future as well as time past. He offers a meditation on the remorseless and intimate involvement of the discrete and individual life in the ever present community of time. Chick's identity is disclosed in the fusion of memory and history that constitutes a moral order—a dimension of being.

Generalizing on my text, therefore, I would say that by implication Gavin Stevens's meditation is writ large in the novels and stories of a company of Southern writers whose careers are substantially to be associated with the generation of the 1920s and 1930s, although notably forecast in certain predecessors, especially in George Washington Cable, Mark Twain, and Ellen Glasgow. I am thinking of William Faulkner, Elizabeth Madox Roberts, Robert Penn Warren, Eudora Welty, Katherine Anne Porter, Andrew Lytle, Caroline Gordon, Allen Tate, Thomas Wolfe. How many others may be called to mind? In the body of stories by these writers we have a struggle of revelation, an effort to achieve a vision of the meaning of the South in terms of the classical-Christian historical order of being in its twofold aspect: the order of being in relation to transcendence; and the order of being in relation to existence in time, of which the future dimension is hidden, and which only God can fulfill. Insofar as this vision is achieved, it in effect constitutes a revelation of meaning which amounts to an almost unique discovery by modern American storytellers of the truth of historical existence. The work of the Southern storytellers constitutes a perception of the difference in the order of being between the transcendent and the mundane. It recognizes that heaven cannot be made immanent; that existence is dualistic in structure, constituting a sacred history and a profane history. I might go even further to assert that the body of Southern fiction I am referring to suggests a reopening of "the hierarchy of being that separates divine from mundane existence." That it suggests to us the possibility (under the dispensation of God's grace) of the "opened soul"; as opposed to the "closure of the soul" (the solipsistic state existent under the secular dispensation dedicated to making the divine immanent).

In referring to the "closure of the soul" I mean the compulsion to the millennial, or Utopian, image of existence in American life in contrast to the small regard for the image of historical reality. My emphasis on this opposition, as may be surmised, derives from an attempt to grasp the significance of Eric Voegelin's analysis of "gnosticism." My grasp of the monumental *Order and History* and of the various books auxilliary to it, including *The New Science of Politics* and *Science, Politics and Gnosticism,* is rough and approximate.[7] These works represent a systematic thought of magnificent sophistication. I apologize for what is undoubtedly a vulgar reduction of Voegelin's concepts.

Simply stated, gnosticism—the record of which is ancient but the major development of which comes with its seemingly irresistible realization in modern science, industrialism, and technology, and in the economic systems these have generated (capitalism and communism) —is the belief that knowledge available to men (gnosis) can be used to change the very constitution of being. "This endeavor," Voegelin has observed, "can be meaningfully undertaken only if the constitution of being can in fact be altered by man. The world, however, remains as it is given to us, and it is not within man's power to change its structure. In order—*not,* to be sure, to make the undertaking possible—but to make it *appear* possible, every gnostic intellectual who drafts a program to change the world must first construct a world picture from which the essential features of the constitution of being that would make the program appear hopeless have been eliminated." [8] In eliminating from a world picture the undesirable elements, the gnostic mind (and Voegelin points out that the gnostic mind and the gnostic general mind merge and are not ultimately truly distinguishable) makes a highly selective evaluation of the past. In extreme gnosticism the past, I suppose, may just be eliminated as a dimension of existence. In any case the gnostic mind concludes (with Hegel) that all history is known to it, up to and including the final culmination which will in some manner be constituted of perfected men in a perfected society. The gnostic approach to history results in an abolition of history, or in the delusion of its abolition. The truth of history—the reality—is that history goes on and on. In our finitude we do not know—and can never know—how the story will end.

Throughout our national history we have tended strongly to idealize the Republic in a gnostic spirit. Having secularized Christian perfectionism and millennialism, we have assumed that we know the end of history; and that this is America, which is the "immanentization of the Christian idea of perfection." In sheer idea—in the most commonly accepted version of the American Dream—America is one of the most alluring fantasies of a new world the gnostic imagination has conceived. Our whole national character, and our existence as individuals, is colored by the assumption that America is "a recreation of being." As we have come into the age of the complete urbanization of American civilization, gnosis, not history, is more nearly than ever before the symbolic form of American life—the great cities sprawling across

Mallison—Lucas Beauchamp dilemma as the situation in a novel because the novel was published at the time after the Second World War when the segregation versus integration issue had begun to be topical. The subject of the relationship of Chick to Lucas, as Lytle indicates, *chose* Faulkner. It constitutes a part of the unfolding in his imagination of the great vision which is the substance of the Yoknapatawpha saga: the historical finitude of the individual Southerner—white, red, black, or of variant hue—under the pressures of the development of the American Republic into the massive industrial democracy of the modern age. In a detachment and loneliness, the extent of which I doubt has ever been understood, Faulkner lived in this vision for nearly forty years, while out of it emerged the lives of all the kinds of people in the American South, from the effective beginnings of the machine age in America, and of the Cotton Kingdom in the South, down to the mid-point of the present century. Emerged, I should declare, mostly in the depiction of characters who are persons in their own right. I want, nonetheless, to emphasize the fact that however much the writer of Faulkner's generation is devoted to the "private lives" of individuals, to their purely personal distinctiveness, he is concerned with their relation to a quest he, the storyteller, is making for an order of memory and history. He conducts this quest because in his generation the Southern literary imagination and talent were chosen to make it. The only other American writers of the twentieth century chosen to pursue such a search, it is instructive to observe with Louis D. Rubin, Jr., have been the American Jewish writers.[9] For this reason Southern fiction and Jewish fiction have been the most complex and vital expressions of American fiction in this century. Both expressions derive from visions in which faith in the American's ability to make his own world has had an entangled confrontation with an experience of memory and history that tells him that he cannot do it. But in the case of the Jewish writer the confrontation involves discrepancies between old and new in which a strongly apprehended traditionalism is a major factor. In the instance of the Southern writer, I doubt that the situation can be so described. When we examine the attractive formula of an Old South traditionalism versus a New South antitraditionalism, it proves to be oversimplified and misleading. The Old South, it has often been said, was a religious and an agrarian society and therefore a traditional order. Early overrun with a divisive and fragmenting Protestantism, the Old South, as Allen Tate pointed out long ago, found no center in the profession of a traditional religion and thus was without a prime requirement of a traditional society. Nor was the Old South, in the usual signification of the term, an agrarian society. Although its main business was agriculture, it was a chattel slave society—a reactionary political economy that found its major symbol in the pastoral and patriarchal plantation but could *conceivably,* in a fuller realization of its essential nature than was permitted by historical circumstances, have found its representation in the industrial slave city. To survive, a reactionary society seeks accommodation to the motives of the action surrounding it. The imagination of the Old South responded to the dynamics of the revolutionary redemption of mankind from the past by the gnostic concepts of modernity. Southerners, for example, spurred by recurrent dreams of perfecting the South as a great tropical slave empire—embracing Mexico, Central America, Brazil, the islands of the Caribbean—transferred the magic of nineteenth-century "American Manifest Destiny" into terms of a "Southern Manifest Destiny." As the Confederacy came into being a Georgia newspaper said with specific reference to the acquisition of Central America:

> This is destiny, and God grant that it may be accomplished without drawing a sword. But it must be accomplished, because Providence designs the spreading out of African slavery into regions congenial and suitable to its prosperity. Such regions are presented in Nicaragua, Honduras, Chihuahua, Tamaulipas in which our omnipotent staples will flourish beneath the plastic hand of black labor. When these golden visions become realities, when we shall feed the nations, as well as supply their looms and spindles, with raw materials, then will the wisdom and prescience of the founders of our new Government be vindicated—then will the proudest nations of the earth come to woo and worship at the shrine of our imperial confederacy.[10]

The golden visions of a Southern Manifest Destiny are echoes in a more general depiction of the destiny of the Confederacy in Henry Timrod's "Ode, on the Meeting of the Southern Congress" (in Montgomery, Alabama, in February, 1861), a poem later called "Ethnogenesis." In this poem the goal of the Cotton Kingdom becomes the complete redemption of poverty throughout the world.

> Could we climb
> Some mighty Alp, and view the coming Time,
> The rapturous sight would fill
> Our eyes with happy tears!
> Not only for the glories which the years
> Shall bring us; not for lands from sea to sea,
> And wealth and power, and peace, though these shall be;
> But for the distant peoples we shall bless,
> And the hushed murmurs of a world's distress:
> For to give labor to the poor,
> The whole sad planet o'er

And save from want and crime the humblest door,
Is one among the many ends for which
God makes us rich! [11]

We wonder how much difference there may be between the Old South's enraptured fantasy of a new world
to come and the New South fantasies in the generation
after the Surrender. The New South, Henry W.
Grady exulted in his memorable speech before the New England Society in 1886, "understands that her emancipation came because through the inscrutable wisdom of
God her honest purpose was crossed, and her brave
armies were beaten." [12] At the same moment Grady had
the notion that "the inscrutable wisdom of God" had
decreed the sacred trinity of education, science, and industrialism to be the salvation of the New South.

The fundamental source of the literary power of the
Faulkner-Lytle-Tate generation, we understand, rises
from the realization of the dialectical quarrel between
the truth of history and the deceptions of gnosis. With
its origins in the Old South as well as the New South,
this quarrel is by no means to be comprehended merely
as opposition between a Southern imagination committed to the historical reality of man's condition and an
outside gnosticism in the North and East. It is to be
understood rather as the far more intimately felt opposition within the twentieth-century Southern literary
mind—a contrariety taking the form not of an ideological
dispute but of a complicated narration and dramatiza-
tion of the desires, hopes, frustrations, and tragedies of
all sorts and conditions of people envisioned as individual human beings trying to survive and, possibly,
to find meaning in a world that both accepts and defies
the reality of history. In some stories, to be sure, the
drama may become transparently ideological. I think it

does in the novels of Robert Penn Warren, who has been called a "philosophical novelist." Everybody recalls Warren's best-known novel, *All the King's Men,* in which there is the juxtaposition of Jack Burden and Cass Mastern. At the beginning of his career as Willie Stark's aide, the modern Southerner Jack Burden has, in Warren's words, no "moral orientation at all that I could figure out"; whereas the antebellum Southerner Cass Mastern (who dies in the Civil War) *"had* faced up to a moral problem in a deep way." [13] The novel turns on Jack's recovery of the past through Cass's discovery of memory and history. When, in the course of a relentlessly pragmatic quest for facts about Judge Irwin's past, Jack finds out that Irwin is actually his father, he becomes aware of what Cass Mastern had discovered through the agonizing acceptance of his moral role in time: the inextricable implication of every human act in the enormous spider web of human actions. Jack moves from regarding the past as a source of useful facts to a vision of the past as mystery and yet a source of moral truth. In the often quoted last line of the story, he goes, he says, "out of history into history and the awful responsibility of Time."

This declaration of Jack's is virtually a condensation of the major theme of the Southern novel of the twenties and thirties. By the time it was spoken (*All the King's Men* was published in 1946), some critics were tentatively assigning an end to what was by then coming to be referred to as a literary renaissance in the South. The conditions which favored the phenomenon, they sensed, were no longer present.

Ten years earlier Allen Tate had described the situation out of which a literary renaissance in the South was developing. His analysis in an essay on "The Profession of Letters in the South" (1935) is familiar:

From the peculiarly historical consciousness of the
Southern writer has come good work of a special order;
but the focus of this consciousness is quite temporary.
It has made possible the curious burst of intelligence that
we get at a crossing of the ways, not unlike, on an in-
finitesimal scale, the outburst of poetic genius at the end
of the sixteenth century when commercial England had
already begun to crush feudal England. The Histories
and Tragedies of Shakespeare record the death of the old
regime, and Doctor Faustus gives up feudal order for
world power.[14]

In 1959 Tate in "A Southern Mode of the Imagination"
offered a refinement of this description, amplifying and
explaining it in retrospect in a discussion of the "particular quality of the Southern writers of our time." The
special quality he finds in the dialectical imagination.
When he says "our time," he refers to the time contemporary with "A Southern Mode . . ." as well as to the
time twenty to thirty years before. Tate, it is clear, was
not in 1959 as impressed by the limited duration of the
Southern achievement as he had been in 1935. No
longer holding it to be "quite temporary," he saw a
renaissance which had persisted for a generation and yet
continued.

But on what terms? According to the application of
Tate's argument I have made, I would say that in 1959
he saw the more or less indefinite focus of the Southern
literary imagination in the opposition that determined
the "peculiarly historical consciousness" of the Southern
writer in the twenties and thirties and on into the forties:
the contention between the truth of history and the com-
pulsions of gnosis. But I think we will ask today, and I
think Tate himself will ask, does this conflict continue
to be central in Southern fiction in the 1950s? The vital-
ity of Southern writing continues, but does it not change

in character? A response to these questions will elaborate on the suggestion I made in the beginning that the Southern Renaissance can be seen as falling into two stages.

To illustrate the nature of the shift in the Southern literary imagination which characterizes the second stage of the Renaissance, I am going to make a limited reference to four works of fiction. All published in the 1960s, they confirm as well the tendencies of the fiction of the 1950s. Two of these are short stories which appear in a collection entitled *Southern Writing in the Sixties: Fiction.* Published in 1966 by the Louisiana State University Press, this volume is intended to be a representative group of stories by (at the time) younger Southern writers. The other works I shall comment on are well known: Robert Penn Warren's novel entitled *Flood: A Romance of Our Times* (1963) and William Styron's *The Confessions of Nat Turner* (1967).

I shall come first to the two short stories. The subject of both is the Southern imagination of memory and history. Both are, I think, very appealing stories; both are about reunions involving persons associated with the Confederacy. One, by John William Corrington, is called simply "Reunion." A recollection of a joint encampment of former Federal and Confederate soldiers at Gettysburg in 1915, it is told by a man who as a small boy had accompanied his grandfather from Milledgeville, Georgia, to the encampment. Seeing his story through the eyes and emotions of the boy, the author controls the story with sympathetic irony. In one part of the story the narrator and his brother, also on the trip, after hearing a speech about the "united North and South" contend for the rightness of their dead grandmother's unreconstructed Southernism as against an attitude of resignation toward the past expressed by the grandfa-

ther. The scene is very skillfully done. But there is one
off-key note, slight but significant. One of the boys says
that he does not "give a hoot in hell" for the Yankee flag.

—Grammaw used to say the red in it was Southern
blood. That the union got fat eating its own people when
they tried to be free. . .
We reached our tent and went inside. Bedford lighted
a kerosene lantern and hung it on the main pole.
—Your grandmother said a lot, grandfather said
wearily. But her text was always the same.
—But . . . , I began.
—Do you want to carry the graves home from here
with you? Do you want to carry the graves inside the
house and set them up there? [15]

Grandfather, we realize, is echoing the famous lines
from Allen Tate's "Ode to the Confederate Dead"
(1927):

What shall we say who have knowledge
Carried to the heart? Shall we take the act
To the grave? Shall we, more hopeful, set up the grave
In the house? The ravenous grave? [16]

Doubting if Grandfather would have anticipated Tate's
poem about the solipsistic modern mind, we cannot but
feel that the otherwise deft portrayal of the old man in
this scene is to some degree impaired when the author
puts a sophisticated literary allusion in his simple mouth.

I would not make too much of this. But the interven-
tion of this allusion in Corrington's story does, I believe,
indicate a condition Southern writers coming into their
literary majority in the 1950s and 1960s could not do
much about: an increasing depletion of the Southern
memory. For two and more full generations after the
Civil War, Southern writers had a resource of memory
in a living link of Southerners. Those who had known

the War, the Surrender, and Reconstruction at first hand were followed by those who had known those who had experienced these events. Writers, like Tate, in other words, possessed a close contact with both an individual and a collective Southern memory. But in the third and fourth generations after the War, the resource of memory began to dissipate.

The second story from *Southern Writing in the Sixties* I want to mention briefly is by Charles East. Entitled "A Tribute to The General," it is a brief, compressed, effective story. Told through the mind of a famous Confederate general's wife, the story describes the last time she goes—not to a literal reunion but to a secondary one, so to speak—a meeting of the Sons and Daughters of the Confederacy in Richmond, Virginia. The time is the 1950s. The old lady in the story has been the second wife of the General, having married him when she was very young and he was an old man. She has spent the years of her marriage aiding the General in his long effort to justify what he did at Gettysburg, a matter of great dispute; and after the General's death, she has spent the better part of a lifetime pursuing the same object. Always in her mind is the image of another woman—the General's first wife, a beautiful woman he loved dearly who had died in childbirth. The second wife, for all her devotion to her husband, knows she has never vanquished the memory of Rose. She also knows something else: that once somewhere the General had said to her, "Sometimes I think we lost because we wanted to." [17]

East has told me how he put "A Tribute to The General" together. General James Longstreet and his second wife, as students of Southern history will know, are the prototypes of the characters. But what suggested the story to East was the persevering appearance of an aged lady before a national committee on the centennial com-

memoration of the Civil War in the early 1960s. A dis-
placed Southerner living in New York, watched over constantly by a black servant, she came to Boston, where the
committee was in session, to attempt to advance the one
purpose she had long had in life: the erection of a statue
of Jefferson Davis in the halls of the national capitol.
Witnessing this pathetic interest on the lady's part, East
recalled a comment written ten years before by General
Longstreet's second wife in regard to a biography of
Longstreet published by the Louisiana State University
Press. In this Helen Longstreet, now quite old—having
spent fifty years since Longstreet's death in 1904 defend-
ing him—bitterly protested the failure of the author, as
she saw things, to give her her proper role in the General's life.

> General Longstreet [she wrote] wooed me to his tent in
> a romance as tender and beautiful as has ever been
> handed down from the courts of King and Chivalry. I
> became more than his wife. I became his Secretary, Nurse
> and adviser. I went everywhere with him. I was never
> absent from his side, one day. I wrote his speeches, kept
> up with his correspondence and helped him revise his
> history of the Confederate war. . . . My face was the one
> that went with General Longstreet into eternity. In the
> delirium of his final hour, his last murmured words were:
> "Helen, we shall be happier at this Post." He had carried
> me back to the Old Army under the flag he loved first
> and loved last. When he died the light of the world went
> out for me. But I lift my eyes to the stars when the road
> is longest and the burden heaviest and again I hear his
> voice in the sweetest tribute the years can render back
> to me: "Helen, you alone have understood me." [18]

Out of the experience of seeing the elderly, unreconstructed lady in New York and of reading Helen Long-

street's remarks, East combined his factual knowledge of
Longstreet's life and wrote his story. Perfectly articulated in substance and tone, there is no jarring note
in it. But like Corrington's story, it documents the depletion of the Southern memory. Subtly elegiac, both stories are memorials of the Southern memory. Both come
out of a contact the writer has with the remembrance of
memory; they render the remembrance of memory, or,
of the memory of memory. Both have their essential
focus in the diminishing power of the great symbols in
the post–Civil War Southern recollection: the Confederate States of America, the War for Southern Independence, the Surrender, and Reconstruction. These are, or
were, the principal orienting events in the "Southern
legend of heroic frustration and defeat," making up the
elements that built in the Southern memory "a City of
the Soul," as Robert Penn Warren has called it.[19] This
collective consciousness of the Confederacy and the Lost
Cause became an ideal homeland of the Southern piety.
In the twentieth-century Southern writer's sensibility it
became the source of a conviction of history as a dimension of the soul and thus the source of his being as a
writer.

Still, if attenuation of the vision of the defeated
Confederacy through the natural process of time would
seem logically to indicate the eventual frustration of the
writer as Southerner, and if Corrington and East keenly
sense the generational diminishment of the Southern
past, their stories do not imply a resistance to the loss
of the Southern identity. The old Confederate soldier
and the ancient Confederate widow are quietly implied
symbols, not of a recovery of history, but of the erosion
of this motive by a cultural process which is no more than
incidentally related to the natural running of time.

The pietistic construct of Southern memory—the

Confederacy as City of the Soul or a spiritual nation—
which arose in the years following Appomattox was
static. It had no genuine literary meaning until it was
transformed by the twentieth-century Southern literary
mind seeking to recover the reality of memory and history—the reality of community—under the aspect of the
mystery of existence as this had been established in the
Hebraic-classical-Christian discoveries of the nature of
the order of being. This effort joined the literary endeavor in the American South to a general renaissance
in Western letters during the age between the First and
Second World Wars. In this age it seemed possible to
a T. S. Eliot, a W. B. Yeats, a Thomas Mann, a William
Faulkner, or an Allen Tate to restore, in the imagination
at least, the temporal and transcendent nature of history
by dramatizing in story, poem, and essay the conflict
between the reality which had long supported Western
civilization and the Faustian dreams of modernity. This
stage in the literary reaction to modernity, it is now clear,
turned toward a conclusion in the 1950s and 1960s. At
the end of the Second World War, European and American writers gravitated toward an emphasis on the intensely personal struggle of the individual to find some
meaning in an absurd and undefinable world. Instead of
the restoration of civilization, the literary mind began to
assume the question of the survival of the integrity of the
individual psyche as a paramount motive. Thus we see
a shifting of the terms of the controlling conflict in the
Southern literary imagination. The struggle between the
moral order of memory and history tends to be transformed into a struggle between a gnostic society and the
existential self. The Southern experience as interpreted
in the imagination of the Southern writer tends to lose
its character as a symbol of the moral order of memory

and history and to become more nearly a symbol of the isolation of the self.

The whole tendency is defined in the progression of Robert Penn Warren's novels after *All the King's Men;* being most graphically revealed in *Flood,* a story in which Warren employs a first-person narrator, Brad Tolliver, who reminds us of Jack Burden. Brad is a writer of real talent, but he has lost "the necessary human connection." His attempt to recover this through recovering in memory and history the meaning of his home town, Fiddlersburg, Tennessee, before it is forever drowned beneath the waters of a gigantic man-made lake, constitutes a story that, whatever its excesses, is one of Warren's most significant works. I cannot go into the intricacies of the story here. Let me only make the point that in it Warren envisions the Southern experience—the Southern white experience—as one not of enveloping community but one of ineffable loneliness. I take one key scene, wrenching it out of a complicated context, to let it stand as indicative of the tendency to imagine the symbolic import of the South in a way different from that of the Faulknerian emphasis. The scene is an old, weed-grown cemetery, where we find Brad Tolliver and his friend, Yasha Jones, a famous Hollywood director, who is to make a movie out of a script Brad is to write about Fiddlersburg. Brad is in search of the grave of Izzie Goldfarb, a long deceased resident of the town. Goldfarb had been a loner, a type of the wandering Jew, a spiritual exile; but in his loneliness, it seems to Brad, a self-contained man. Brad thinks of him as somehow being a key to the signification of Fiddlersburg. Extending his reflections on Goldfarb into a general declamation on the theme of loneliness in the South, Brad declares: "Hell, the whole South is lonesome. It is as lonesome as coon hunting, which has always been a favorite sport, and that is lonesomer than anything except frog-gigging on a dark night in a deep pond and your skiff leaking, and some folks prefer it that way." Brad continues: "Hell, the South is the country where a man gets drunk just so he can feel lonesomer and then comes to town and picks a fight for companionship." The Confederate States, he says, "were founded on lonesomeness." And he moves on to an explicit repudiation of the concept of the South as a community. The "shared experience . . . that makes the word *South,"* he tells Yasha, is "lonesomeness": "Hell, no Southerner believes that there is any South. He just believes that if he keeps on saying the word he will lose some of the angry lonesomeness. The only folks in the South who are not lonesome are the colored folks. They may be angry but they are not lonesome." [20]

The heart of the race problem, Brad observes, is the envy the white folks have of the black sense of community. This is why, he says, referring to an earlier part of the story, the white people in the town have been so keenly anticipating that a black convict now awaiting execution in the state prison, which looms on a hill above Fiddlersburg, will break down and pray before his final moment. They want him to "crack and pray because . . . if a man prays you know he is took lonesome. That's why they want that black boy to pray." Continuing in this vein, Brad asserts that Southerners pray but not because they believe in God. They believe in "the black hole in the sky God left when He went away." Brad asks Yasha to look at the black hole in the sky. When Yasha remarks that he sees nothing, perhaps because he does not believe in God, Brad brings his harangue to a close.

"I don't believe in God," Brad said. "And I don't believe in the black hole in the sky either." He paused.
"What I believe in," he said, "is Fiddlersburg."

"Fiddlersburg," Yasha Jones murmured. Then asked,
softly: "So that is why you are back here?" [21]

As the story unfolds in *Flood* and Brad tries with
progressive desperation to make Fiddlersburg come
alive in his imagination, it becomes apparent that he is
trying to attain his salvation by giving himself a personal
moral identity. Although he does not succeed, he comes
to the point of some possibility of doing so. But the point
is not that reached by Jack Burden, who is on the verge
of being able to accept a responsibility for living under
the limitations of the mystery of time, or a responsibility
for the meaning of history. *Flood* ends with Brad looking
upon the last days of Fiddlersburg and thinking that he
has failed to trust "the secret irrational life of man" and
for this reason has not found *"the connection between what
I was and what I am . . . the human necessity."* He has
learned: *"There is no country but the heart."* [22] There may
be hope in this. And yet Brad's quest tends toward a
solipsistic conclusion: to make a meaning of being is an
act of self-salvation. To disclose the self in the community of history—we ask with Brad at the end of his story
if this is a credible possibility.

At the conclusion of *Flood* we are no longer in the
presence of a faith in a redeeming moral order of memory and history, which, when fully apprehended (recov-
ered) in the consciousness, reveals the presence of the
past in all human affairs, showing forth the human necessity between what *was* and what *is*. The reduction of faith
in the redemptive power of the moral order of memory
and history is more strikingly dramatized in *The Confes-*

*sions of Nat Turner,* a novel that, I would say, shares with
*Flood* the distinction of being the most provocative fiction
by a Southern writer in the 1960s. Based on a careful
fictionalization of the famous slave rebellion in South-
ampton County, Virginia, in 1831, this novel, Styron says
in an introductory note, intends "to re-create a man and
his era, and to produce a work that is less an 'historical
novel' in conventional terms than a meditation on history." [23] In this last respect it is not remarkably different
in its treatment of history from that we find in writers
of the earlier period of the Southern Renaissance.
Faulkner, Lytle, Tate, Caroline Gordon—all are medita-
tors on history more than imitators of it as in the case
of conventional historical novelists. But Styron's meditation on history in *Nat Turner* is distinguishable from all
prior meditations by Southern writers. For one thing, the
meditation is directly expressed by a first-person narrator; and the meditator-narrator, Styron's persona, is an
antebellum black, a chattel slave. He is, moreover, a narrator who, save in that he lacks his sophistication, is
endowed by virtue of a rather extreme fictional license
with the skill and power of a gifted and trained modern
writer like Styron. Indeed he writes in Styron's style.
Since his great capacity with words is not commensurate
with his very limited education—he is both consum-
mately literate and intellectually naive—Nat achieves a
wide range of ironic nuance as he tells his story, and a
considerable intricacy of suggestion develops in the
course of the novel. Not the least interesting suggestion
is that Nat bears a relation to the figure of the modern
man of letters and that his "confessions" have a connection with the "confessional literature" of modern literary
history. From Rousseau to Robert Lowell this literature
records the striving to authenticate the existence of the
writer as a person, as against the deprivation of the self

constantly threatened by society. Placing Nat in the context of the confessional writings, we glimpse the modern myth of the writer as a redemptive hero. At the same time we cannot miss the fact that Nat is located in a definite time and place; and that as a figure of the man of letters, if he is taken as such, he represents the first direct emergence in Southern, or for that matter, in American literature of the suppressed figure of the gardener (the slave) from the antebellum garden of the chattel. In his ironic identification with Nat's consciousness, Styron may be making a daring effort to extend the dimensions of the Southern recovery of memory and history to a recovery of the mind of the slave. He would make this almost voiceless and virtually unknown mind a part of the past that is the present.

And yet in his intriguing conception of Nat as the articulate voice of the gardener speaking at last from the garden in which the imagination of the masters of the Old South had enclosed him, Styron does not seek to express the integral relationship of the past and present. He uses the garden of the chattel and Nat's role in it as an illustration of the contemporary world. Nat's contemplative discourse is devoted not to the subject of a possible recovery of the past. It is a meditation by a mind implicated in a society fallen into inner intellectual and spiritual chaos because it has been dispossessed of the reality of memory and history—and so of the reality of human community—by a gnostic modernity. Nat's implicit recognition of his metaphorical identity as a figure of the latter-day twentieth-century world and of the import of his lengthy meditation on the meaning of his life can be traced throughout the novel. But it is intimated most precisely and cogently in the affinity Nat perceives between himself and Jeremiah Cobb, the judge who sentences him to death. Cobb is a drunkard, a ruined Jeffer-

sonian, a man of rational and humane education who has
been completely dispossessed of the dream of Virginia
as an errand into paradise. His witness to the violation
of the dream occurs in a scene in which Nat recalls how,
although in accents of stinging mockery, Cobb covertly
approves of Nat's reputed ability to read—a skill which,
Cobb declares, makes Nat "not a thing but a *person.*" Nat
remembers Cobb's having exclaimed as he clutched a
brandy bottle and looked madly at a distant line of trees
thrashing in the wind:

> God, God, my poor Virginia, blighted domain. The soil
> wrecked and ravaged on every hand, turned to useless
> dust by that abominable weed. Tobacco we cannot any
> longer raise, nor cotton ever, save for a meager crop in
> these few southern counties, nor oats nor barley nor
> wheat. A wasteland! A plump and virginal principality,
> a cornucopia of riches the like of which the world has
> never seen, transformed within the space of a century to
> a withering, defeated hag! And all to satisfy the demand
> of ten million Englishmen for a pipeful of Virginia leaf!
> Now even that is gone, and all we can raise is horses!
> Horses! . . . Horses and what else, *what else?* Horses and
> pickaninnies! *Pickaninnies!* Little black infants by the
> score, the hundreds, the thousands, the tens of thou-
> sands! The fairest state of them all, this tranquil and
> beloved domain—what has it now become? A *nursery* for
> Mississippi, Alabama, Arkansas. A monstrous breeding
> farm to supply the sinew to gratify the maw of Eli Whit-
> ney's infernal machine, cursed be that blackguard's
> name! In such a way is our human decency brought
> down, when we pander all that is in us noble and just to
> the false god which goes by the vile name of *Capital!* Oh,
> Virginia, woe betide thee! Woe, thrice woe, and ever
> damned in memory be the day when poor black men in
> chains first trod upon thy sacred strand! [24]

Nat first sees Judge Cobb, and hears his despairing lament of the defeat of the golden apocalypse Virginia had held forth, when he is still on the Turner plantation and some distance away from his rebellion. But he is already under the command of an apocalyptic errand: he has been chosen by God to free his people. The plan that unfolds to Nat calls for him to lead a small band of his fellows in the destruction of all the white people in and around Jerusalem, Virginia, then flee into the Dismal Swamp to await a general slave uprising. Eventually, two years or more later, during an eclipse of the sun (witnessed by Nat after five days of fasting and wrestling with his soul in the woods) the revelation of Nat's commission from God becomes complete. After this Nat recalls how he had told his followers that "the seal had been removed from my lips and I had received the last sign. I said that the spirit had appeared to me in the form of an eclipse of the sun, which they themselves had witnessed. The Spirit had informed me that the Serpent was loosened and Christ had laid down the yoke he had borne for the sins of men. I went on patiently to explain that the Spirit had commanded that I should take on the yoke and fight against the Serpent, for the time was fast approaching when 'the first shall be last and the last shall be first.' " [25]

It is plain that Cobb's despairing apocalypse and Nat's vision of violent redemption in Styron's novel are ironically apposite. The defeat of the dream of Virginia as a paradise by a ruthless materialism of money, machines, and slaves forecasts the inevitable defeat of a millennial New Jerusalem of freed slaves. The dreams originate in the same source: the false conception of redeeming the human condition through, as it were, an engrafting of the human will on the mystery of history.

In a sense Nat realizes this when Judge Cobb sentences him to be hanged; and in this inexplicable moment Nat realizes too that his moment of truth is shared by Judge Cobb, who is himself near death. "We gazed at each other over vast distances, yet close, awesomely close, as if sharing for the briefest instant some rare secret—unknown to other men—of all time, all mortality and sin and grief." [26] But what Nat realizes that he paradoxically shares with Cobb is the knowledge of the radical and mortal loneliness of each individual existence. This knowledge Nat has gained experientially under the conditions of life in the time and place he knows as the American South. It is a knowledge of a loneliness more definitive, more final, than that Brad Tolliver in *Flood* discovers in the life of the South. Nat not only repudiates the notion that in the Old South the master class and the slaves existed in pastoral amity, but Brad's notion that, if the whites in a later South are lonely and unhappy, at least the blacks are full of pastoral community and at peace with themselves. Rebuking these clichés, Nat suggests, more deeply, a repudiation of the idea that the literary imagination of the South can properly employ the South as a symbol of the community of memory and history.

Nat is a willed creation of a post-Faulkner, post-Tate storyteller. Nat could not have taken over Faulkner's mind, for Faulkner would not have willed him to be. Faulkner conceived the individual as a summation of the past. "There is no such thing really as was, because the past is," he once said. "It is a part of every man, every woman, and every moment. All of his or her ancestry, background, is all a part of himself and herself at any moment. And so a man, a character in a story at any moment in action, is not just himself as he is then, he is all that made him." [27]

I do not mean to schematize *The Confessions of Nat Turner*. Styron if far more a storyteller than a conceptualist, so that in his total novel about Nat there is a medley of conflicts and undoubtedly these reflect a disharmony that, like life, defies conceptual patterning. For instance, Nat's love for Margaret Whitehead, the only person Nat kills during the rampage of the slaves through the Virginia garden, may conceivably redeem him from his isolation. But the fulfillment of his love of Margaret occurs in the sexual rapture of an imagined union in the last moments before he is conducted to the scaffold. In the same instant of rapture Nat experiences a union with the Lord Jesus. He does not, it would appear, truly experience the grace of a divine identity beyond himself. We cannot escape concluding that Nat's long meditation on history is at heart ironically a meditation on the intimacy and ecstasy of the existential self, fulfilled at the last in a totally subjective, an autistic, experience.

The twentieth-century literary mind was directed toward the recovery of memory and history as long as it accepted, or deeply wanted to accept, the value system of the Christian-humanist civilization of the West, in which the primacy of memory and history is central. With acceptance failing, the Southern literary mind has turned toward continuing the striving with a gnostic modernity through the idea of the self as the constitutive realm of being—the source of its possibilities and its limitations. The covenant with memory and history has been abrogated in favor of a covenant with the existential self. Faulkner's works, we may say, attempted a ratification of the first covenant, Styron's attempt the ratification of the second. However necessary this second endeavor may be, and however courageous, it is an act of dispossession. It dispossesses the South of Faulkner—that large and

# Notes

## ONE—*The Garden of the Covenant and the Garden of the Chattel*

1. *The Puritans,* ed. Perry Miller and Thomas H. Johnson (New York: American Book Company, 1938), p. 198.

2. The association between the image of the New Jerusalem and the Garden of Eden was close. See Stanley Stewart, *The Enclosed Garden: The Tradition and the Image in Seventeenth-Century Poetry* (Madison: University of Wisconsin Press, 1966), pp. 13–31.

3. *American Literature: The Makers and the Making,* ed. Cleanth Brooks, R. W. B. Lewis, and Robert Penn Warren (New York: St. Martin's Press, 1933), I, 31. Only the translation of the Latin or Ramus is quoted.

4. *The Wall and the Garden: Selected Massachusetts Election Sermons, 1670–1775,* ed. A. W. Plumstead (Minneapolis: University of Minnesota Press, 1968), pp. 204–5, 210.

5. Ibid., pp. 61–64.

6. Ibid., pp. 152–53.

7. Ibid., p. 149.

8. Ibid., p. 168.

9. Ibid., pp. 172–73.

10. Ibid., pp. 29–30.

11. Ibid., p. 129.

12. See Robert Penn Warren's introductory essay to his *John Greenleaf Whittier: An Appraisal and a Selection* (Minneapolis: University of Minnesota Press, 1971), pp. 3–61.

13. Jonathan Edwards, "Personal Narrative," in *Representative Selections,* ed. Clarence H. Faust (New York: American Book, 1935), p. 69.

14. Henry Adams to Brooks Adams, September 8, 1895, *Letters of Henry Adams, 1892–1918,* ed. Worthington Chauncey Ford (New York: Houghton Mifflin, 1938), II, 80.

15. "The Public Garden," in *American Poetry,* ed. Gay Wilson Allen, Walter B. Rideout, James K. Robinson (New York: Harper and Row, 1965), pp. 1005–6.

16. "Religion and Society in Early Virginia," in *Errand into the Wilderness* (New York: Harper and Brothers, 1964), p. 119.

17. Ibid., p. 140.

18. *The History and Present State of Virginia,* ed. Louis B. Wright (Chapel Hill: University of North Carolina Press, 1947), pp. 298–99. Cf. Leo Marx, *The Machine in the Garden: Technology and the Pastoral Ideal in America* (New York: Oxford University Press, 1964), pp. 75–88.

19. Beverley, *History of Virginia,* p. 5.

20. Pierre Marambaud, *William Byrd of Westover, 1674–1744* (Charlottesville: University Press of Virginia, 1971), pp. 146–47.

21. *Slavery: A Problem in American Institutional and Intellectual Life* (Chicago: University of Chicago Press, 1968), pp. 37–38.

22. Marambaud, *William Byrd,* pp. 171–72.

23. *Virginia Magazine of History and Biography,* ix (January 1902), 234–35.

24. Marambaud, *William Byrd,* p. 147.

25. Sartre, *What Is Literature?* (New York: Washington Square Press, 1966), pp. 67–68.

26. William Cohen, "Thomas Jefferson and the Problem of Slavery," *Journal of American History,* lvi (December 1969), 503–26.

27. Ibid., 518.

28. *Notes on the State of Virginia,* ed. William Peden (Chapel Hill: University of North Carolina Press, 1955), pp. 137–43.

29. Ibid., pp. 162–63.

30. Ibid., pp. 164–65. The ironic historical relationship between the growth of slavery and the independence of the yeoman farmers in Virginia is instructive with regard to Jefferson's mind. See Edmund S. Morgan, "Slavery and Freedom," *Journal of American History,* lix (June 1972), 5–29.

31. The discussion and quotations are drawn from Karl Lehmann, *Thomas Jefferson: American Humanist* (New York: Macmillan, 1947), pp. 179–81.

## TWO—*Slavery and the Culture of Alienation*

1. Charles Baudelaire, *The Essence of Laughter and Other Essays, Journals, and Letters* (New York: Meridian Books, 1956), p. 188. Baudelaire's remark is placed in a more elaborate context than can be developed here in Lewis P. Simpson, "The Southern Writer and the Great Literary Secession," in *The Man of Letters in New England and the South: Essays in the History of the Literary Vocation in America* (Baton Rouge: Louisiana State University Press, 1973), esp. pp. 230–35.

2. Ibid., esp. pp. 235–41.

3. Quoted in "Introduction" to *The Variorum Walden,* ed. Walter Harding (New York: Washington Square Press, 1963), p. xiv.

4. John Taylor, *Arator, Being a Series of Agricultural Essays, Practical and Political* (Petersburg, Va.: Printed by Whitworth and Yancey for John M. Carter, 1818), no. 29, pp. 190, 189.

5. Ibid., no. 13, p. 48.

6. Russell Kirk, *Randolph of Roanoke: A Study in Conservative Thought* (Chicago: University of Chicago Press, 1951), p. 12.

7. Ibid., p. 154.

8. Ibid., p. 163.

9. William R. Taylor, *Cavalier and Yankee: The Old South and American National Character* (New York: Doubleday, 1963), pp. 162–64.

10. *Swallow Barn; or, A Sojourn in the Old Dominion* (New York: G. R. Putnam, 1854), pp. 21–22.

11. Ibid., p. 461.

12. Ibid., pp. 459–60.

13. Ibid., pp. 461–90.

14. Ibid., p. 11.

15. Ibid., pp. 470, 483.

16. "The Proslavery Argument Reconsidered," *Journal of Southern History,* xxxvii (February 1971), 3–18.

17. Simms to Charles L. Wheler, May 9, 1849, *The Letters of William Gilmore Simms,* ed. Mary C. Simms Oliphant, Alfred Taylor Odell, and T. C. Duncan Eaves (Columbia: University of South Carolina Press, 1953), ii, 515.

18. Simms to James Henry Hammond, May 20, 1845, *Letters,* ii, 65.

19. Simms to James Henry Hammond, December 24, 1847, *Letters,* ii, 386.

20. Simms to John Esten Cooke, April 14, 1860, *Letters,* ii, 215.

21. Simms as quoted in J. V. Ridgely, *William Gilmore Simms* (New York: Twayne, 1962), pp. 22–24.

22. *Uncle Tom's Cabin; or, Life among the Lowly,* with an Introduction by Howard Mumford Jones (Columbus, Ohio: Charles E. Merrill, 1969), ii, 179, 213. A facsimile of the first printing; two volumes in one.

23. Ibid., ii, 143.

24. Ibid., ii, 15, 217.

25. *Woodcraft; or, Hawks about the Dovecote: A Story of the South at the Close of the Revolution* (New York: J. S. Redfield, 1854), p. 114.

26. Ibid., p. 509.

27. Ibid., pp. 509, 518.

28. *The World the Slaveholders Made: Two Essays in Interpretation* (New York: Pantheon Books, 1969).

29. Simms to John William Bockee, December 12, 1860, *Letters,* iv, 302.

30. *Woodcraft,* pp. 508–19. I am indebted in general to this provocative study.

## THREE—*The Southern Recovery of Memory and History*

1. "The Fall of the House of Usher" in *Complete Works of Edgar Allan Poe,* ed. James A. Harrison (New York, E. R. Dumont, 1902), ii, 280, 286.

2. Peter Gay, *The Enlightenment: An Interpretation* (New York: Vintage Books, 1968), p. 271.

3. William Faulkner, *Intruder in the Dust* (New York: Modern Library, c. 1948), pp. 194–95.

4. Andrew Lytle, "Regeneration for the Man," in *The Hero with the Private Parts* (Baton Rouge: Louisiana State University Press, 1966), p. 132.

5. Ibid.

6. Allen Tate, "A Southern Mode of the Imagination," in *Essays of Four Decades* (Chicago: Swallow Press, 1968), p. 592.

7. Three volumes of *Order and History* have been published: *Israel and Revelation, The World of the Polis,* and *Plato and Aristotle* (Baton Rouge: Louisiana State University Press, 1956, 1957). A fourth volume is forthcoming. Also, see *The New Science of Politics: An Interpretation* (Chicago: University of Chicago Press, 1952): *Science, Politics, and Gnosticism* (Chicago: Henry Regnery, 1968).

8. *Science, Politics, and Gnosticism,* p. 100.

9. Louis D. Rubin, Jr., "The Experience of Difference: Southerners and Jews," in *The Curious Death of the Novel* (Baton Rouge: Louisiana State University Press, 1967), pp. 262–81.

10. The Macon *Daily Telegraph,* February 28, 1861, quoted in Robert E. May, *The Southern Dream of a Caribbean Empire, 1854–1861* (Baton Rouge: Louisiana State University Press, 1973), p. 238.

11. Henry Timrod, *Collected Poems,* ed. Edd Winfield Parks and Aileen Wells Parks (Athens: University of Georgia Press, 1965), pp. 94–95.

12. "The New South," *The Literature of the South,* ed. Thomas Daniel Young, Floyd C. Watkins, and Richmond Croom Beatty, rev. ed. (Glenview, Ill.: Scott Foresman, 1968), p. 482.

13. Ralph Ellison, William Styron, Robert Penn Warren, and C. Vann Woodward (moderator), "The Uses of History in Fiction," *Southern Literary Journal,* I (Spring 1969), 77. Edited transcript of a panel discussion, Southern Historical Association, New Orleans, November 6, 1968.

14. Allen Tate, "The Profession of Letters in the South," in *Essays of Four Decades,* pp. 533–34.

15. John William Corrington, "Reunion," in *Southern Writers in the Sixties: Fiction* (Baton Rouge: Louisiana State University Press, 1966), pp. 184–85.

16. *The Literature of the South,* ed. Young, Watkins, Beatty, p. 755.

17. Charles East, "A Tribute to The General," in *Southern Writing in the Sixties: Fiction,* p. 51.

18. Files of the Louisiana State University Press.

19. Robert Penn Warren, *The Legacy of the Civil War: Meditations on the Centennial* (New York: Vintage Books, 1964), p. 14.

20. Robert Penn Warren, *Flood: A Romance of Our Time* (New York: New American Library, 1965), pp. 143–44.

21. Ibid., p. 144.

22. Ibid., p. 367.

23. "Author's Note," *The Confessions of Nat Turner* (New York: Random House, 1967), [p. 9].

24. Ibid., pp. 68–69.

25. Ibid., p. 349.

26. Ibid., p. 106.

27. *Faulkner in the University,* ed. Frederick L. Gwynn and Joseph L. Blotner (New York: Vintage Books, 1965), p. 84.

# Index